VANISHED CHURCHES
OF THE
CITY OF LONDON

Gordon Huelin, PhD, FSA

CORPORATION
OF LONDON

Guildhall Library Publications

Corporation of London
Guildhall Library Publications
Guildhall Library
Aldermanbury
LONDON EC2P 2EJ

ISBN 0 900422 42 4

First published 1996

Printed in Great Britain by
The Balkerne Press Limited

FOR MEG
WHO OVER THE YEARS
HAS SHARED IN MY
CITY DISCOVERIES

St Olave Jewry, in the
preceding its demolition

iv

CONTENTS

FOREWORD

Its churches are one of the great glories of the City of London. Not only do they form an architectural heritage, unrivalled perhaps other than by the churches of Rome, they also bear witness to the concern that this most commercial of cities had for its spiritual welfare. Not many people are aware that so many churches were destroyed over the centuries. It is this gap in general knowledge of the City which Dr Huelin has sought to fill.

There could be no better qualified person to do this than Gordon Huelin. An historian and writer of note, he is also a clergyman who was, for many years, Guild Vicar of St Margaret Pattens in Eastcheap and Chaplain to the Mercers' Company, the senior livery company of the City.

In this book he gives the reader a detailed insight into the history of all the churches which were destroyed by the Great Fire of 1666 and thereafter. It is a real treasure trove of information and I thoroughly commend it to all lovers of the City and its history.

Alderman Sir Alexander Graham, GBE
(Lord Mayor 1990-91)

PREFACE

More than a quarter of a century ago I wrote a booklet on *The Pre-Fire City Churches*, namely the thirty-five places of worship that were not rebuilt after 1666. I tried there, as far as was possible, to guide readers to discover for themselves what could still be found relating to those churches by way of records, burial-grounds, City Corporation plaques and so on. However, such have been the changes which have occurred in the "Square Mile" between then and now that the original publication badly needed bringing up to date.

When undertaking this task, I was invited to extend the scope of the work to include the other vanished City churches: first, the considerable number demolished between the latter part of the eighteenth century and 1939; and second, those which perished during World War II and were not restored. It is my hope that readers will again be moved to set forth on a voyage of discovery — even though they will find it longer than the previous one. I should like here to express thanks to Dr Peter Galloway both for the encouragement he has given me and for compiling the list of parish boundary marks which forms the Appendix. This has involved much time and effort on his part.

Guildhall Library — a veritable treasure-house which has provided me with material and pleasure since boyhood days — is in the fortunate position of being in possession of the archives of *all* the churches featuring here. The fact that such documents survive is due in no small measure to the conscientious churchwardens and other officials who, even after their own church disappeared, ensured that its records were preserved and sent to a place where they could be properly kept. Stephen Freeth and Irene Gilchrist, senior members of Guildhall Library, kindly read my manuscript and provided valuable comments. Jeremy Smith spent many hours in helping me to choose illustrations from its incomparable collection. Alan Day gave painstaking help in the production of the map. In fact, without the assistance of the Library's staff, it would have been impossible to carry out this assignment.

To have the "Foreword" written by my friend and fellow-Mercer, Alderman Sir Alexander Graham, is indeed a privilege. David Beasley, Librarian of the Goldsmiths' Company, gave information concerning Holy Trinity Gough Square, and James Bentley of the RIBA particulars concerning some architects and City churches now destroyed. Joe Wisdom, the Librarian of St Paul's, supplied details of church plate now in the Cathedral Treasury, and Commander John Stevens, Clerk to the Wax Chandlers', of St John Zachary's silver on loan to that Company. Simon Smith, who is in charge of Guildhall Library Publications, has been of great help in seeing the book through its various stages. To all these, and especially to the Corporation of London for its generosity in publishing it, I am immensely grateful.

Gordon Huelin
Feast of the Transfiguration 1995

VANISHED CITY CHURCHES

Numbers shown thus ( ) refer to the map opposite and the entry number in the text.

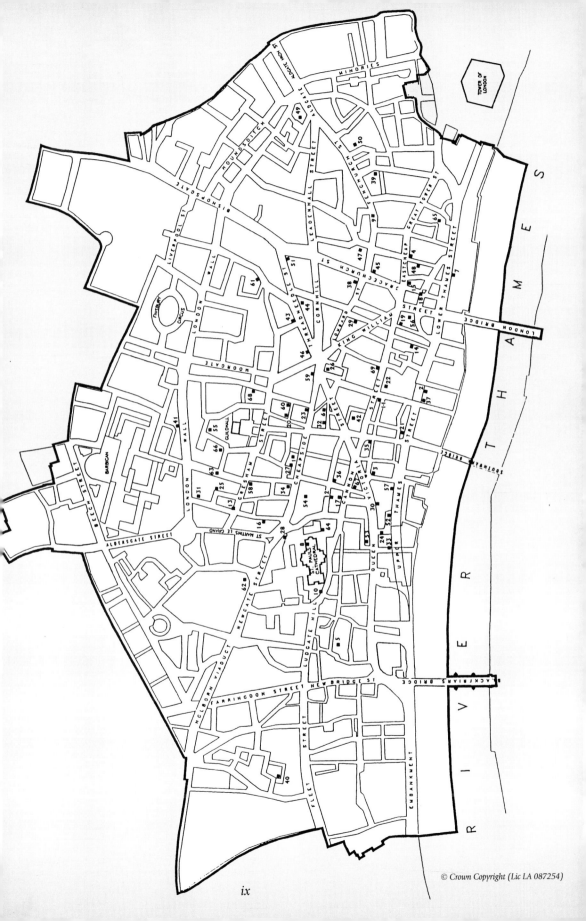

© Crown Copyright (Lic LA 087254)

ix

I
Churches Not Rebuilt After the Great Fire of 1666

Until the middle of the seventeenth century the City's skyline was dominated by more than a hundred church spires and towers, presenting what must have been an unforgettable sight. Many of these churches and their parishes, however, were extremely small in size. The Great Fire of 1666, in which eighty-nine churches were destroyed, afforded an opportunity for the replanning of the City; and whatever form this was eventually to take, it should have been obvious to everyone that a considerable number of those churches would never rise again. Indeed, if the City authorities and Christopher Wren, who was in charge of the rebuilding, had been allowed to have their way, the restored City, instead of retaining its old parishes, would have been apportioned into only thirty-nine new ones. But the demands of citizens prevailed and an Act passed in 1670 laid down that fifty-one of the destroyed churches were to be rebuilt. This meant that over thirty would vanish entirely, their parishes being united with neighbouring ones, though they would continue to be represented by churchwardens and parish clerks. The parishes particularly affected by this legislation were those in the centre of the City and notably around Cheapside where, before the Fire, some churches had almost adjoined each other. When it came to the question of union with another parish, personal preferences were sometimes ignored by the authorities — as, for example, the request of the parishioners of St Mary Colechurch to be united with St Martin Pomary rather than with St Mildred Poultry. The decision not to rebuild St Gabriel Fenchurch, which had stood in the middle of a main street and even then doubtless caused some traffic problems, may be appreciated; but it is difficult to understand why St Laurence Pountney, with its historic associations and before the Fire one of the tallest spires in the City, should have been allowed to vanish. At least its attractive churchyard still remains.

1.   **ALL HALLOWS HONEY LANE**

This church, which stood north of Cheapside almost opposite the Standard, was in existence before 1235. John Norman, Draper, and Mayor in 1453 — the first Mayor to go in state to Westminster by water — was buried in its chapel. To visit the rectory in Henry VIII's reign incurred suspicion, for the parish priest during the 1520s, Dr Forman, was known to hold Lutheran opinions and his one-time curate, Thomas Garret, who became rector in 1537, suffered martyrdom at Smithfield as a heretic. The parish was a small one; only five died of the Great Plague. After the Fire it was united with St Mary le Bow, the church site being occupied by Honey Lane Market. A few shops known by this name survived until World War II. Today the site of both church and market is covered by offices. A bee carved in stone above the

entrance to Honey Lane in Cheapside gives a reminder of what was probably the particular commodity sold in this area of old London's main market-place. There are parish boundary marks in Cheapside. An almsdish, given to All Hallows in 1660 by Maurice Walrond, can be seen in the St Paul's Cathedral Treasury.

2. **ALL HALLOWS THE LESS**

In the part of Thames Street formerly called the "Ropery", from the fact that ropes were made and sold here, there stood two churches, both dedicated to All Hallows. The smaller one, All Hallows the Less, was known from the days of Henry III as "above the cellars", since it stood on vaults. The steeple and quire were built over an arched gate which was the entrance to a large house named Cold Harbour. In the sixteenth century the quire collapsed, but Stow referred to it as having been newly restored at the parishioners' cost in 1594. Some thirty years later, further repairs called for their generosity, and to lighten the gloomy interior dormer windows were then inserted on the south side. Following the burning of the church in 1666, the parish was joined to All Hallows the Great. The churchyard of All Hallows the Less and City Corporation plaque marking the church site disappeared some years ago with the building of Mondial House in Upper Thames Street. An old watch-house, with a recess for a handbell, had already been destroyed during World War II. According to an inscription at the centre of an almsdish in St Paul's Treasury, this "Bason" was remade in 1708 for All Hallows, partly from plate given by Lady Anne Glover and partly from old plate belonging to the parish.

3.   **HOLY TRINITY THE LESS**

To distinguish it from the priory of Holy Trinity, Aldgate, the only ancient parish church in the City with the same dedication was called "the Less". The earliest reference seems to be in 1266. Stow speaks of it as "very old". He adds that it was in danger of falling down and that although collections had been made towards necessary repairs these had proved insufficient, the church being then supported by props. It was rebuilt in 1606–7 with the help of further contributions from individuals, as well as from nearly all the other City parishes. The churchwardens' account book dating from 1582 contains a full list of these, and of the work of rebuilding. There is even a "black list" of those parishes which gave no help! Several accounts commence with fine pictorial letters, one of which is illustrated here. From answers to the Royal Commissioners' enquiries in 1552, it appears that there belonged to the church fifteen "Robin Hood coats", presumably used by actors in parish plays. Henry Machyn, who kept a valuable sixteenth-century diary, was a parishioner. He records how Thomas Chambers, rector in 1559, became involved in a brawl and hit a young man on the head with a bottle. As a result, Chambers found himself first in the Compter and then in Bridewell. The parish was annexed to St Michael Queenhithe after the Fire. A church for foreign Lutherans later occupied the site until the construction of Mansion House Station. A City Corporation plaque marking the site of Holy Trinity church in Little Trinity Lane has gone, but there is a parish boundary mark in Great Trinity Lane.

4.   ST ANDREW HUBBARD

Until a few years ago a City Corporation plaque on No. 16 Eastcheap stated that in the roadway opposite formerly stood the church of St Andrew Hubbard. Its distinctive surname probably came from Hubert, a medieval benefactor. When excavations took place here in 1836, traces of Roman work were seen in the church foundations and fragments of Samian pottery were unearthed. These suggested that St Andrew's was erected on what had once been a Roman building. The churchwardens' accounts are some of the earliest in the City and are particularly valuable as giving a continuous record of parish life from 1454. They present a lively picture of the fifteenth-century church: with the woman keeping her fruit-stall at its door, the gatherings of its members in Eastcheap on festival days and its sufferings from rats for whom it was necessary to purchase "beytte". After the Fire the parish was united with St Mary at Hill. The King's Weigh House was then built on the site. Part of this was occupied by a Nonconformist meeting-house which became known as the King's Weigh House Chapel and remained here till last century. Parish boundary marks can be found in Philpot Lane and Talbot Court.

5.   ST ANN BLACKFRIARS

First mentioned in 1544 as "the parish of St Ann within the site of the Friars Preachers", though considerably older, this was situated close to Church Entry, Carter Lane. When in 1550 the priory precinct was granted to Sir Thomas Cawarden, he pulled down St Ann's along with the church formerly belonging to the Black Friars. The St Ann's site he leased out for tennis courts and its burial ground he converted into a carpenter's yard. In Mary's reign he was com-

The Remains of the Ancient Church of Saint Ann Blackfriars

pelled to find another building where the parishioners could worship and gave them "a lodging in a chamber above a stair". When this fell down in 1597, the congregation raised enough money within a year to rebuild it and later on, more to enlarge it. It became a noted Puritan stronghold and large numbers came here from all over the City. Many visitors to London felt their itinerary incomplete unless they had attended a lecture at Blackfriars. Playhouse Yard is a reminder of the association of the parish in Elizabethan and Stuart times with the Blackfriars Theatre, a relationship not of the happiest nature since, according to a petition drawn up by the inhabitants of the Blackfriars' precinct in 1596, the noise of drums and trumpets disturbed the church services. In any case, the plays produced there would have been uncongenial to the Puritanically-minded members of St Ann's. After 1666 the church was amalgamated with St Andrew by the Wardrobe. Two portions of its churchyard remain: one in Church Entry and the other in Ireland Yard. The latter contains part of the wall of the former Blackfriars' priory.

6. ST BENET SHEREHOG

The name of this church, which formerly stood at the north end of Sise Lane, presents a puzzle. Originally it was dedicated to a Saxon martyr, St Osyth. Then, according to Stow, in the reign of Edward II, Benedict Shorne, a "stock-fishmonger", rebuilt the church, driving out the patron saint and giving it instead his own name which became altered to "Sherehog". Should this be the case, it is somewhat ironical that while the church of the intruder has now vanished, the original saint is still remembered in "Sise" — a corruption of "St Sithe's" — Lane. William Sawtre, a curate here at the beginning of the fifteenth century and a convert to Lollard opinions, was the first to suffer martyrdom for "heresy" at Smithfield in 1401 under an Act passed that year. On 22 February 1591/92 was born, in Sise Lane, Nicholas Ferrar, founder of a religious community in Huntingdonshire, at the hamlet of Little Gidding known now to many through T.S. Eliot's *Four Quartets*. Nicholas's father repaired and reseated St Benet's and at his own expense engaged a Sunday preacher. Despite the church's past associations and monuments, it was not rebuilt after 1666, the parish being united with that of St Stephen Walbrook. The small churchyard of St Benet remained in Pancras Lane until the autumn of 1994, but was then, unhappily, sacrificed for the redevelopment of No. 1 Poultry. According to a report in *The Times* of 2 August 1995, excavations on its site revealed that Roman tiles and stones had been used in the eleventh century to build the church walls, part of which were still standing. A replica of the plaque in the illustration included here could be seen until recently on a building adjoining the churchyard. One hopes that it may be replaced when the present work is completed.

7. ST BOTOLPH BILLINGSGATE

"A proper church and hath had many fair monuments," says Stow, of a building of very early foundation. The fact that Botolph's Gate, later known as Botolph's Wharf, is mentioned in the time of William the Conqueror, suggests that the church was already in existence and gave the Wharf its name. St Botolph was, according to some authorities, the patron of travellers, and so had several churches dedicated to him near the City gates, this one being not far from the gateway to old London Bridge. Stow indicates that the "fair monuments" once here were, by his day, "all destroyed by bad and greedy men of spoil". The vestry minutes, dating from 1592, record that in 1647 during the Commonwealth period, the parishioners took part in an election for a new minister. After the Fire the parish was united with St George, Botolph Lane. During the early 1980s, excavations were undertaken by members of the Museum of London's department of urban archaeology in the Billingsgate Lorry Park. These revealed medieval remains of St Botolph's including a well-preserved undercroft. A City Corporation plaque which marked the church's site has disappeared, but part of what was formerly the "upper burying ground" survives between Nos 31 and 35 Monument Street.

8. ST FAITH UNDER ST PAUL'S

This stood on the north side of old St Paul's until 1255. Then, when the cathedral was lengthened, the church was pulled down, the parishioners being given as their place of worship the west end of the crypt under St Paul's quire. The east section of the crypt, separated by a screen, became the Jesus Chapel. Stow says that in Edward VI's reign the parish church of St Faith was removed to this chapel which was "more sufficient for largeness and lightness". In 1666, as the Fire spread westwards, the parishioners, most of whom were stationers or booksellers in Paternoster Row, stored their books for safety in their church below the Cathedral. According to Pepys, sparks from other goods stacked in the churchyard outside penetrated the windows of St Faith's so that its roof collapsed and more than £150,000 worth of books perished. Subsequently the parish was joined to St Augustine, Watling Street. The crypt chapel of St Paul's is still known as St Faith's Chapel. A pump with the inscription "Erected by St Faith's Parish 1819" stands in a recess beside the Cathedral Chapter House in St Paul's Churchyard. A parish boundary mark is on the wall of the Choir School in New Change.

9. ST GABRIEL FENCHURCH

A map of pre-Fire London shows this as on an island site in Fenchurch Street, rather like the churches in the Strand today. It was in existence before 1321. Stow says the title "Fen" was derived either from the marshy ground on which the church was built, or from the word "foenum" (Latin = "hay") from the nearby haymarket in Gracechurch Street. Pepys records that in the afternoon of Sunday April 9 1665, he went to "the little church in the middle of Fenchurch Street" where were "very few people". After 1666 the parish was united with St Margaret Pattens and, until the rebuilding of the latter, the combined congregations worshipped in a temporary structure erected in St Gabriel's churchyard. Its entrance was by way of Tabernacle Alley which still existed on the north side of Fenchurch Street till the middle of the present century. On the wall of Plantation House, Fenchurch Street, a City Corporation plaque indicates that the church of St Gabriel's stood in the roadway opposite. A paved portion of the churchyard is in Fen Court and contains three tombs, two belonging to the Cotesworth family. Dr Cotesworth's name appears in an early eighteenth-century list of subscribers towards the new church plate then purchased for the use of the united parishes.

10. ST GREGORY BY ST PAUL'S

This stood at the south-west corner of old St Paul's near where is now Queen Anne's statue. Its dedication to the pope responsible for St Augustine's mission to England suggests an early foundation. During the Danish ravages of East Anglia in 1016, the body of the martyr-king Edmund was brought here from the local shrine for safety till the danger was over. The church was rebuilt with the cathedral after the latter had been destroyed by fire in 1087. When, in Elizabeth I's reign, St Paul's steeple was struck by lightning, the cathedral services were temporarily held in St Gregory's. Its nearness to St Paul's proved a mixed blessing, for when the seventeenth-century architect Inigo Jones undertook the cathedral repairs, he began to pull down St Gregory's to the annoyance of the parishioners. The vestry minutes of 1646–7 give details of the rebuilding work and its cost. Evelyn notes in April 1654 that he heard the Caroline divine, Jeremy Taylor, preach a sermon at St Gregory's "concerning evangelical perfection". The Prayer Book services, though generally forbidden during the Commonwealth period, continued to be used here by the rector Dr John Hewitt. Hewitt's correspondence with the royalists led to his arrest and execution on Tower Hill in 1658. Following the Fire, the parish was united with St Mary Magdalen, Old Fish Street. Apart from records in Guildhall Library, no memorial of St Gregory's remains.

11.   ST JOHN THE BAPTIST UPON WALBROOK

Stow says this was aptly named, since its west end stood by Horseshoe Bridge on "the very bank" of the Walbrook. The earliest reference to the church appears to be in the twelfth century. It was rebuilt in 1412, and repaired in 1621 and again in 1649–50. According to the churchwardens' accounts, the sum paid in 1621 "to several workmen and for several sorts of stuff" for repairing the church and churchyard was just over £104. Thirty years later the repairs cost more than £1,160. After 1666 the parish was amalgamated with St Antholin Budge Row. A tiny portion of its former churchyard remains in Cloak Lane. This contains some tombstones and a monument inscribed to the effect that when, in 1884, the formation of the District Railway necessitated the destruction of most of the churchyard, the human remains were collected and reinterred in a vault beneath. On the side wall a tablet commemorates the church site. First set up in 1671, it was newly faced and the letters fresh cut in 1830. There are parish boundary marks in Walbrook, Cannon Street, Dowgate Hill and College Street.

12. ST JOHN THE EVANGELIST FRIDAY STREET

This parish, south of Cheapside, was the smallest in the City, covering less than an acre. Most of the medieval parishioners were fishmongers who had premises in Friday Street, so called because Friday was the fish-market day. The church was one of the thirteen "peculiars" in the City belonging to the Archbishop of Canterbury. It seems originally to have also been dedicated to a Saxon princess, St Werburga. It was repaired in 1626 and a gallery was then added, possibly for the benefit of those who came to listen to the Rev. George Walker, rector 1614–50. He published numerous sermons and books setting forth his Puritan views. Laud described him as a "disorderly and peevish man". St John's had the distinction of being the only parish in which there were no deaths from infection during the Great Plague of 1665. The church was not so fortunate in the disaster of 1666 and the parish was afterwards joined to All Hallows, Bread Street. Until World War II, the south side of Watling Street was brightened by St John's churchyard at the corner of Friday Street. Both the churchyard and this part of Friday Street have since been absorbed in the building development of this area. A City Corporation plaque can be found beneath the arch of No. 1 Watling Street.

A generall Bill for this present year,
ending the 19 of *December* 1665. according to
the Report made to the KINGS most Excellent Majesty.

By the Company of Parish Clerks of *London*, &c.

Parish	Buried	Pla.	Parish	Buried	Pla.	Parish	Buried	Pla.	Parish	Buried	Pla.
St Albans Woodstreet	200	121	St Clements Eastcheap	38	20	St Margaret Moses	38	20	St Michael Cornhill	104	52
St Alhallowes Barking	514	33c	St Dionis Back-church	78	27	St Margaret Newfish	114	66	St Michael Crookedla.	179	133
St Alhallowes Breadst	35	16	St Dunstans East	265	150	St Margaret Pattons	49	24	St Michael Queenhit	203	122
St Alhallowes Great	455	426	St Edmunds Lumbard.	70	36	St Mary Abchurch	99	54	St Michael Que-ne	44	18
St Alhallowes Honila	10	5	St Ethelborough	195	106	St Mary Aldermanbury	181	109	St Michael Royall	152	116
St Alhallowes Lesse	239	175	St Faiths	104	70	St Mary Aldermary	105	75	St Michael Woodstreet	122	62
St Alhall. Lumbardstr.	90	62	St Fosters	144	105	St Mary le Bow	64	36	St Mildred Breadstreet	59	26
St Alhallowes Staining	185	112	St Gabriel Fen-church	69	39	St Mary Bothaw	55	30	St Mildred Poultrey	68	46
St Alhallowes the Wall	500	356	St George Botolphlane	41	27	St Mary Colechurch	17	6	St Nicholas Acons	46	28
St Alphage	271	115	St Gregories by Pauls	376	232	St Mary Hill	94	64	St Nicholas Coleabby	125	91
St Andrew Hubbard	71	25	St Hellens	108	75	St Mary Mounthaw	56	37	St Nicholas Olaues	90	62
St Andrew Vndershaft	274	189	St James Dukes place	262	190	St Mary Summerset	342	262	St Olaves Hartstreet	237	160
St Andrew Wardrobe	476	30	St James Garlickhithe	189	118	St Mary Staynings	47	27	St Olaves Iewry	54	32
St Anne Aldersgate	282	19	St John Baptist	138	83	St Mary Woolchurch	65	33	St Olaves Siluerstreete	250	132
St Anne Blacke-Friers	652	467	St John Euangelist	9		St Mary Woolnoth	75	38	St Pancras Soperlane	30	15
St Antholins Parish	58	33	St John Zacharie	85	54	St Martins Iremonger	21	11	St Peters Cheape	61	35
St Austins Parish	43	20	St Katherine Coleman	299	213	St Martins Ludgate	196	128	St Peters Cornehill	136	76
St Barthol. Exchange	73	51	St Katherine Creechu.	335	231	St Martins Orgars	110	71	St Peters Pauls Wharfe	114	86
St Bennet Fynch	47	2	St Lawrence Iewry	94	48	St Martins Outwitch	60	34	St Peters Poore	79	47
St Benn. Grace-church	57	41	St Lawrence Pountney	214	140	St Martins Vintrey	417	349	St Stevens Colmanst.	560	391
St Bennet Pauls Wharf	355	172	St Leonard Eastcheap	42	27	St Matthew Fridaystr.	24	6	St Stevens Walbrooke	34	17
St Bennet Sherehog	11	1	St Leonard Fosterlane	335	255	St Maudlins Milkstreet	44	22	St Swithins	93	56
St Botolph Billingsgate	83	50	St Magnus Parish	103	60	St Maudlins Oldfishstr.	176	121	St Thomas Apostle	163	110
Chrifts Church	653	467	St Margaret Lothbury	100	66	St Michael Bassishaw	253	164	Trinitie Parish	115	79
St Christophers	60	47									

Buried in the 97 Parishes within the walls, — 15207   Whereof of the Plague — 9887

13. **ST JOHN ZACHARY**

According to a twelfth-century deed, the canons of St Paul's gave the church of St John the Baptist to the monk Zachary. It was subsequently given his name to distinguish it from St John the Baptist, Walbrook. In 1181 an investigation produced a list of ornaments belonging to the church. Henry de Spondon, a wealthy medieval rector, rebuilt it at his own expense. In the fifteenth century two churchwardens were dismissed from the office for misconduct, while a priest was charged with being an habitual drunkard. Machyn tells of the 1559 Midsummer Day festivities in the parish, consisting of "a giant and drums and guns and the Nine Worthies, with speeches and a goodly pageant, with a queen crowned, and divers others with speeches; and then St George and the dragon, the morris dance, and after Robin Hood and Little John and Maid Marian and Friar Tuck". In the seventeenth century the church was enlarged. The churchwardens' accounts record that in 1613, at the burial of a former Mayor, Sir James Pemberton, one of the bells broke and hastily had to be mended with a bedcord. They also give the expenses incurred in pulling down part of the steeple after the Fire. The parish was then amalgamated with St Anne and St Agnes. Part of the ruins of St John's remained until last century. The churchyard, at the corner of Gresham Street and Noble Street, is now incorporated in a garden provided by the Goldsmith's Company which had close links with the pre-Fire building. A City Corporation plaque marks the site. Another Company associated with the church were the Wax Chandlers, who held their election service there from 1547 until 1666 and have a Hall

opposite. Various items of silver belonging to St John Zachary, including Elizabethan and Jacobean Communion cups and patens, have been on permanent loan to this Company since 1974.

14.   **ST LAURENCE POUNTNEY**

Early in the fourteenth century, Sir John Poultney, Draper and Mayor, built beside the church of St Laurence, Candlewick Street, the chapel of Corpus Christi and College of St Laurence Poultney (later corrupted to Pountney), as is recorded by a City Corporation plaque. In the reign of Edward III the weavers of Flanders held their meetings in the churchyard. The church stood between the present Laurence Pountney Hill and Lane, north of the passage which joins them. It was an imposing building with battlements and a tall steeple which in old views towers above other City spires. The manner in which this steeple perished in 1666 led some to suppose that a fire was deliberately started there. Malcolm in his *Londinium Redivivum* says: "The tall spired steeple of St Laurence Pountney was then afire, which appearing first at the top discovered itself with so much terror, as if taking a view from that lofty place of what it intended sud-

S. Lorentz Poultney

denly to devour." Pepys writing on September 2 1666 refers to the poor steeple "whereof my old school-fellow Elborough is parson, taken fire in the very top and there burned till it fell down". Subsequently, St Laurence was united with St Mary Abchurch. Two open spaces remain, the church ground and churchyard. The vestry minutes show the parishioners' concern for their up keep. So, there was an order in 1681 that no clothes should be dried in the church ground; in 1711 that Mr Long's cock and hens should not be in the church ground or churchyard; in 1727 that "a falling down post with a crossbar be put up in the middle of the passage to prevent horses going through"; and in 1791 that servants should not beat carpets against the tomb-stones. Despite changes this corner is still one of the most attractive in the City.

15. ST LEONARD EASTCHEAP

First mentioned in 1214, this was also known as "Milke Church", from one William Melker, "an especial builder thereof". The name of William Melker of Eastcheap appears in the Calendar of Wills towards the end of the thirteenth century. When Mary became queen, the rector of St Leonard's, John Tourner, was deprived and forced to do penance because he had married. The steeple was damaged by fire in 1618 and had to be rebuilt and at the same time the church was enlarged. Donations raised outside the City helped to meet the expenses incurred. This must have been one of the first churches to perish in 1666. It was later joined to St Benet Gracechurch. A small churchyard remained until last century. On No. 2a Eastcheap is a City Corporation plaque marking the church site. A sixteenth-century stone tablet, formerly attached to the wall of St Leonard's vestry and now in the Museum of London, bears a quaint inscription concerning the rebuilding of the vestry in 1584. After the Fire this tablet was built into the wall of a cellar in Eastcheap and plastered over. It would have been forgotten had it not been for the vigilance of the parish officers, who demanded that the wall be pulled down till it was found.

16. ST LEONARD FOSTER

Mentioned first in the thirteenth century, this stood on the west side of Foster Lane. Stow recalls a monument to Robert Trappis, Goldsmith, of 1526, inscribed with a curious epitaph pleading that although the Trappis family may be forgotten "when the bells be merrily rung, and the mass devoutly sung, and the meat merrily eaten", yet they may remain in the memory of Christ. With the destruction of the collegiate church of St Martin le Grand in Edward VI's reign and the building of new tenements on its site, St Leonard's parish was much increased. The church was consequently enlarged. In the early 1640s its rector, William Ward, charged with being "innovating and scandalous", was forced to resign. He had apparently preached against the Scots. Ward fled to Oxford, where he is said to have died of starvation. Archbishop Laud, then a prisoner in the Tower, eventually, against his will, agreed to the appointment of a successor. After 1666 the parish was amalgamated with Christ Church, Newgate Street. For a short time during the nineteenth century the General Post Office occupied the church site. This is marked by a City Corporation plaque in Foster Lane. A St Leonard's Communion cup of 1616 is now at St Sepulchre's Holborn.

17. **ST MARGARET MOSES**

This church, which stood at the south end of Friday Street was, according to Stow, so called "of one Moyses that was founder or new builder thereof". A twelfth-century deed belonging to St Paul's indicates that Moyses was a priest. John Rogers, the first Protestant martyr to suffer under Mary Tudor, was for a short time rector in 1550. A sixteenth-century churchwardens' account book (see my article in *Guildhall Studies in London History*, vol.1, no.1, October 1973) contains some curious items: as in 1554 following Mary's accession to the throne, when two pence were spent on "a dispelling rod" — perhaps used for sprinkling holy water? That such religious changes were short-lived is clear from Henry Machyn's *Diary*, where reference is made to a funeral service here in January 1559 for one of the masters of Christ's Hospital, at which John Jewel, the newly-appointed Bishop of Salisbury, preached and "said plainly that there was no purgatory". Following the church's destruction in the Great Fire, the parish was united with that of St Mildred Bread Street. A City Corporation plaque, marking the site on No. 20 Cannon Street, disappeared during rebuilding after World War II. A paten, or dish, formerly belonging to St Margaret's, bearing the 1624 hallmark and inscribed with the date of the gift, 1631, is in the Museum of London.

18. **ST MARGARET NEW FISH STREET**

In medieval London this church, dating from before 1190, must have been prominent on the main roadway to and from old London Bridge and would have been familiar to pilgrims. This may explain the unusually varied collection of relics which, according to an inventory of 1472 now in the "Book of Saint Margaret New Fish Street" in Guildhall Library, were among the church's treasures. They included portions of "the manger or crib that our Lord Jesus Christ was laid in", "the bush of Moses", "the rod of Moses wherewith he divided the Red Sea", "the stone whereon Mary Magdalene did her penance" and "the clothing of St Mary the Mother of Christ Jesus". Beside these "a tooth of St Brigid" seems almost commonplace! Bishop John Alcock, founder of Jesus College, Cambridge, possibly drew up the list, for he was rector here 1461–71. It was generally known as St Margaret, Bridge Street, and appears thus in two City Ordinances: one of 1311 requiring lampreys from France to be set out for sale under the church wall immediately on arrival in this country; the other of 1379 mentioning the conduit beneath the wall as one of the two places where fresh fish could be sold. The church being the nearest to Pudding Lane, where the Great Fire began, must have been the first to suffer destruction. It was subsequently united with St Magnus. The site is now covered by the Monument. Boundary marks remain and there is a City Corporation plaque on Lloyds Bank, Nos. 11–15 Monument Street.

19. ST MARTIN ORGAR

In the twelfth century, St Martin's Candlewick Street was given to the canons of St Paul's by Orgar, the deacon, and later took his name. William Crowmer, Mayor in 1413, built a chapel on the south side and was buried there. He left bequests for church repairs and for the poor, and his name frequently occurs in the churchwardens' accounts. These date from 1471 and include a list of gifts collected in 1574 for the poor in Christ's Hospital. In the seventeenth-century vestry minutes appears the signature of Brian Walton who became rector in 1628. A Laudian in outlook, Walton upset his Puritan parishioners and they petitioned for his removal. In 1641, charges were published wherein Dr Walton's "subtle tricks and Popish innovations are discovered". He then retired to Oxford to work on the Polyglot Bible for which he became famous. Though damaged by the Fire, the church was not entirely destroyed. The parish was, however, united with St Clement Eastcheap. According to the vestry minutes of December 8 1671, the gift of £100 from Mrs. Diana Alington towards the restoration of St Martin's was then to be used for clearing the ground for a Tabernacle to be built with pews and seats; as well as for the casting of the bell-metal into a new bell (to hang in the tower which had survived). For many years the building was used by French Protestants, but by the 1820s it had fallen into a ruinous condition and both church and tower were then pulled down. They were replaced by a new tower in the Italianate style, with a projecting clock dated 1853, still to be seen in Martin Lane. A City Corporation plaque also marks the site.

20. ST MARTIN POMARY

Halfway along Ironmonger Lane, north of St Olave's Court, stood St Martin Pomary. Its distinctive surname is now thought to have come from a benefactor. Stow believed it was derived from apples growing nearby – it is fascinating to imagine an apple-orchard near Cheapside! However, his further remark "I myself have seen large void places" supports another theory, that it came from a Latin word meaning "an open space near the Roman wall". In medieval times the patronage was in the hands of the prior of St Bartholomew the Great, Smithfield. St Martin's was one of the places where the Reformation got off to too early a start, for in 1547 the rector and churchwardens without authority removed the images, set up the royal arms in place of the crucifix, and painted the walls with scriptural texts "whereof some were perversely translated". They excused themselves on the grounds that the roof had so decayed that it was in danger of falling in, while the crucifix and images had on removal crumbled to dust. They were bound over in the sum of £20 a head, and ordered to erect a new crucifix. In 1627 much of the north wall had to be rebuilt. After 1666 the parish was joined to St Olave Jewry. An eighteenth-century boundary mark is illustrated above, and may be seen on the wall beside Mercers' Hall in Ironmonger Lane. Part of the open space leading to the old tower of St Olave's was formerly St Martin's graveyard.

21. ST MARTIN VINTRY

Prior to the widening of Upper Thames Street in the 1960s there was, at the corner where it joins Queen Street, the churchyard of St Martin Vintry, then sacrificed for the construction of the nearby Whittington Garden. Numerous documents witness to the church's early foundation. In one it is referred to as St Martin "Bare-mannechurch". The latter word comes from an old English term signifying "porter" or "bearer". It was one of the earliest titles of St Martin's and suggests that the church was originally erected for those engaged in the extensive wine trade of this neighbourhood. Before the dissolution of the monasteries the patronage was in the hands of the Abbot and convent of St Peter,

 Gloucester. About 1299 St Martin's was rebuilt by the executors of a Bordeaux wine-merchant, Sir Matthew de Columbars. In the fifteenth century it was given a new timber roof covered with lead. This is clearly shown in the "copper-plate map" of the City dated c.1559, and, as John Schofield points out, is confirmed by documentary evidence. It is known that the church had a peal of five bells, but the statement sometimes made that the ancient Society of College Youths had its beginnings here is merely a conjecture. After the destruction of St Martin's in the Fire, the parish was joined to St Michael Paternoster Royal. A parish boundary mark survives on the south side of Upper Thames Street.

22. ST MARY BOTHAW

About 1150, Peter the priest gave his church of St Mary "Bothage" to Canterbury Cathedral. It became one of the thirteen "peculiars" in the City belonging to the Archbishop. Among distinguished parishioners was London's first Mayor, Henry Fitz Ailwyn, who died in 1212 and had an imposing monument. Robert Chicheley, Mayor in 1422, also buried here, provided in his will that every year on his birthday a good dinner should be given to 2,400 poor men of the City and each should also have two pence. Stow writes: "Midway betwixt London Stone and Walbrook corner, is a little lane with a turnpike in the midst thereof, and in the same a proper parish church called St Mary Bothaw, or Boathaw". He explains the surname is derived from a nearby "haw" or yard where boats were made or landed from the harbour of Dowgate to be mended. A small cloister adjoined the church. By Stow's time most monuments had been defaced and the brasses removed. After the church's destruction in 1666, an order was made that its walls and steeple should be taken down and the material used in rebuilding St Swithin London Stone, with which the parish was then united. Part of St Mary's burial-ground with a section of the east wall of the church, remained until Cannon Street Station was built last century. Parish boundary marks are to be found in Cannon Street, Dowgate Hill and Walbrook. St Mary's has the noteworthy distinction of being the only church in the United Kingdom, other than St James Garlickhithe (also in the City of London), whose registers begin before 1539, the official year of registration. The originals, which include Christenings, Marriages and Burials from 1536, are kept in Guildhall Library's department of manuscripts, where they can be examined on microfilm.

23. ST MARY COLECHURCH

According to Stow, this was "named of one Cole that builded it", and was constructed on a vault above ground-level, the entrance to it being up a flight of steps. Peter, the chaplain of St Mary Colechurch in the 1170s, was the builder of old London Bridge. He dedicated a chapel on the bridge to the martyr Thomas Becket, who had been baptised in St Mary's. In 1447, a grammar school was set up in the parish under the charge of John Neel, rector of Colechurch and Master of the Hospital of St Thomas of Acon in Cheapside. When the latter was suppressed under Henry VIII, the Mercers' Company became patrons of St Mary Colechurch. Following the destruction of St Mary's in the Great Fire, the Company was granted an application to purchase the church ground, and there built the new Mercers' School which was opened in 1672 and remained here till 1787. The Company's Acts of Court reveal that in December 1669, some of the parishioners of St Mary's appeared before a committee, requesting to be united with St Martin Pomary rather than with St Mildred Poultry which, they said, "is perpetually disturbed with the noises of carts and coaches, and wants sufficient place for burials". Nevertheless, the union with St Mildred's eventually went through. When the bodies were removed from the pre-Fire St Mary's, it was discovered that they had simply lain between the church floor and the arches on which it was built. On the corner of Old Jewry a City Corporation plaque marks the church site. A parish boundary mark of 1690 on the wall beside Mercers' Hall in Ironmonger Lane, and next to one of St Martin Pomary, is illustrated.

24. ST MARY MOUNTHAW

This small church was originally a chapel belonging to the Mounthaunt family from whom it took its name. It stood at about the middle of the present Lambeth Hill. In the nineteenth century the house of the Mounthaunts, together with their chapel, by that time a parish church, was bought by Ralph de Maidstone, Bishop of Hereford. For many years the Bishops of Hereford used this "Inn" as their London residence. One of them, John Skip, a theologian of some repute, was buried in St Mary's. Thomas Thrall, its rector from 1630–43, was deprived on charges of not preaching or catechizing on Sunday afternoons, of drunkenness and swearing and of bowing to the altar. After the Fire the parish was joined to the nearby St Mary Somerset. The site of St Mary Mounthaw remained as a burial ground until the construction of Queen Victoria Street absorbed it and nearly all the rest of the parish. An eighteenth-century tablet, formerly on the wall of a building in Lambeth Hill, denoting parish property, disappeared during World War II.

25.　ST MARY STAINING

This was one of two churches bearing the name "Staining". It used to be said that this was derived either from the painter-stainers living in the parish, or from the Saxon word for stone — this being one of the few City churches to be built of that material. Modern authorities however, connect the word with a family from Staines who owned property in the neighbourhood of St Mary's. The church is first mentioned in 1189. Before the dissolution of the religious houses the patronage belonged to the convent of Clerkenwell. The church was the scene of violence in 1278 when one Richard de Codeford, accused of robbery, having fled here for sanctuary, struck his pursuer with a lance through a hole in the window and killed him. Samuel Austin, rector in 1665, was one of the few City clergy who remained and died at his post during the Great Plague. He was succeeded by Israel Tongue, later remembered as the ally of Titus Oates in discovering the celebrated "Popish Plot". After the Fire the parish was joined to St Michael, Wood Street. A garden with some tombstones remains in Oat Lane, beside Pewterers's Hall, and modern lettering on the wall attests that it is "St Mary Staining Churchyard". An old tablet commemorating the church site perished in World War II.

26.　ST MARY WOOLCHURCH HAW

In the heart of the City, where Mansion House now stands, was a building of early foundation, St Mary Woolchurch Haw. Its curious name came from a beam in the churchyard where wool was weighed until the latter part of the fourteenth century. In 1442, when St Mary's was found to be "old and feble" and in need of reconstruction, consideration had to be given to the needs of the expanding Stocks Market which stood beside it. Hence the new north wall of the church was built some fifteen feet away from the Stocks Market so as not to obstruct its light. Stow described the church as "reasonably fair and large" and mentioned its curiously-made, painted and gilded font. On September 6 1657, Evelyn records that he heard a sermon from "a grave old man at Woolchurch on Psalm 102, v.6, showing the ignominy of Christ's sufferings". Thomas Langley, churchwarden at the time of the Fire, was one who deserves to be specially remembered for devotion to duty: for, as is recorded in a memorandum in the fine volume of churchwardens' accounts, so intent was he on saving his church's treasures that he left his own belongings to perish in the flames. After 1666, St Mary's was united with the neighbouring St Mary Woolnoth. Its site was first occupied by an open market, named in old maps as Woolchurch Market. This survived until 1737 when the Mansion House was built. In the then excavations a stone was found bearing a consecration cross and the name of John Sturgeon, a distinguished citizen of the fifteenth century when the church was reconstructed. A City Corporation plaque on Mansion House marks the church site.

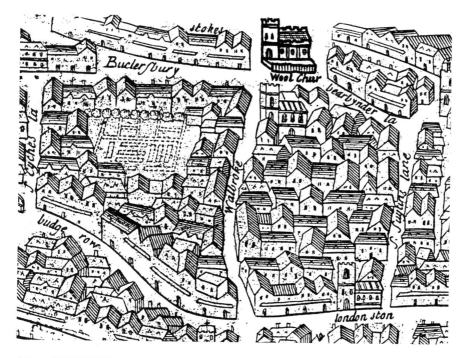

27. **ST MARY MAGDALEN MILK STREET**

This was in existence in the twelfth century. Though Stow refers to it as "a small parish church", the number of Mayors and other notable citizens buried within its walls suggest that it was an important one. Milk Street, which took its name from the produce sold there, is known to have been a distinguished residential quarter. In the early seventeenth century the church had a bell-tower on top of the steeple: for, in the vestry minutes of January 9 1648/49, it was ordered that the lantern in which the little bell hangs be taken down since "the wind having great power on it, it is an occasion to do prejudice unto the church". Anthony Farindon, a royalist divine and a noted preacher, became rector in 1647. During his time the congregation so increased that it was difficult to find room and this became known as "the scholars' church". Evelyn records that on May 7 1654 at Milk Street church, Jeremy Taylor preached on the danger of the contempt of small sins. Farindon was deprived in 1656, being succeeded by Thomas Vincent, a Nonconformist who later wrote a graphic account of the Plague and Fire. The latter destroyed St Mary Magdalen which was subsequently annexed to St Lawrence Jewry. The site became part of Honey Lane Market, and later in the nineteenth century was occupied by the City of London School. A City Corporation plaque in Milk Street commemorates the site of the school, but not of the church. Parish boundary marks may be found in Cheapside.

28. ST MICHAEL LE QUERNE

Close to Paternoster Row, north-west of the Cathedral, stood St Michael ad Bladum, or at the Querne, so called from a nearby market where corn was sold. There was a right of way through the old church during daylight hours. In 1378 the rector and others attempted to put an end to this by blocking up the doorway with a stone wall. The Mayor, Aldermen and Sheriffs then paid a visit to St Michael's, and having seen the obstruction, ordered the culprits to remove it or pay a fine of £20 each. Before 1390 there stood at the east end the old Cheapside Cross, but this was taken down and replaced by a water conduit. In 1430 the church was rebuilt and enlarged. Among monuments was one to John Leland, "Father of English antiquaries" and author of the *Itinerary*, buried here in 1552. Ralph Treswell's survey of 1585 includes the elevation of St Michael's church, with conduit and tall wooden buckets nearby. Sir Thomas Browne, who wrote the *Religio Medici*, was baptised here in 1605. The church-wardens' accounts date from 1514. They record that in July 1666, Matthew Rycroft, churchwarden, received one bond of £150 and various items of church plate. A year later, he was able to hand over all these intact to his successor, together with some church furnishings, one "black cope" and four ancient books — a fine testimony to the integrity of a warden whose church meanwhile had been destroyed. In 1669, when the church was united with St Vedast, Foster Lane, several parishioners "taking into consideration the ruinous condition of the parish church being burned down, and the great want of a convenient place to meet in for the worship of God", contributed £75 towards a temporary place of worship within the old St Michael's walls. A parish boundary mark can be seen on the Cathedral Choir School in New Change.

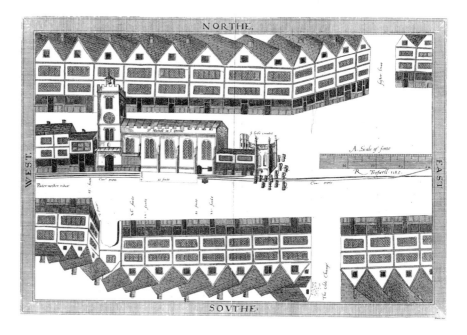

29. **ST NICHOLAS ACONS**

In Nicholas Lane just south of Lombard Street was St Nicholas Acons, or Hacons. Excavations on the site in 1964 revealed fragments of Saxon pottery and the foundation walls of a church clearly dating from within a short period of the Norman Conquest. In 1084 it was given by one Godwyn to Malmesbury Abbey on behalf of himself and his wife "for the redemption of their souls and the remission of their sins and of all Christians". It probably took its surname from an early benefactor Hacon, a name fairly common in medieval London. According to Stow, John Bridge (or Brugge), Mayor in 1520, furnished the church with battlements and was later buried there. After 1666 the parish was united with St Edmund, Lombard Street. Though the church perished, its register book of 1539 escaped. Entries include the baptism in 1585 of "a manchild a foundling named Nicholas Acon after our parish church name". Until recent rebuilding in Nicholas Lane the churchyard was still in existence. Frequent items as to its upkeep occur in the vestry minutes. A City Corporation plaque in Nicholas Lane marks the site of St Nicholas' parsonage, where Scientific Life Assurance began in 1762; while a one time fire-plug at the foot of a building in the lane, opposite Nicholas Passage, has on it "E & S Poynder London St NA 1836".

30. **ST NICHOLAS OLAVE**

Situated where until after World War II was Bread Street Hill but is now Senator House, Queen Victoria Street, was St Nicholas Olave. It is described by Stow as "a convenient church". The word "Olave" was thought to have been derived from "Olaf", some Danish benefactor, but according to Mr C.L. Kingsford, came about through the union in 1250 of St Nicholas with St Olave, Bread Street, the latter then being given by Henry III to the Austin Friars as their London home. By its association with the Scandinavian saint, St Nicholas was one of the few examples of City churches with a double dedication. The parish was inhabited by merchants, cheesemongers and fishmongers. Many were buried in the church, as was also William Blitheman, organist and Gentleman of the Chapel Royal during the reign of Elizabeth I. A note in Kingsford's edition of Stow's *Survey* contains the epitaph on his monument, which included the lines:

"Of Princes' Chapel Gentleman
    Unto his dying day,
Where all took great delight to hear
    him on the organs play".

In the churchyard were five almshouses, the inhabitants of which were supported by the Ironmongers' Company. After 1666 the parish was joined to St Nicholas Cole Abbey. A City Corporation plaque marked the church site, but with its disappearance every trace of St Nicholas Olave has gone.

31. **ST OLAVE SILVER STREET**

Where Noble Street joins London Wall is the churchyard of St Olave, Silver Street, a building dismissed by Stow as "a small thing and without any monuments". It is mentioned in 1181 as "St Olave de Mukewellstrate", from its proximity to Monkwell Street — one of several streets to disappear as the result of post-war redevelopment in this area. The fact that Silver Street was in medieval times the home of the London silversmiths may explain why the figure of Christ on the rood in the pre-Reformation church was decorated with silver shoes. Machyn, writing on July 29 1557, says that this "being St Olave's day was the church holiday in Silver Street; and at eight of the clock at night began a stage play of a goodly matter that continued until twelve midnight and then they made an end with a good song". Dr Boosey, who was rector when the Civil War broke out in the seventeenth century, is said to have been so abused by the rebels that he died of grief. The church records mention a foundling named Olave Silver. After the Fire, the parish was united with St Alban, Wood Street. Set in the wall at the churchyard entrance is the curious stone tablet illustrated here.

32.   **ST PANCRAS SOPER LANE**

This church, first mentioned in 1257, was, as recent excavations have revealed, a simple building with an apse at the east end. Soper Lane is today part of Queen Street, while Needlers Lane in which the church formerly stood is now called Pancras Lane. Although a small building, the church had the support of various wealthy parishioners. Such an event as the wedding between William Relff, of the parish of St Bartholomew the Less, and Colly Malory, daughter of Mr Alderman Malory of this parish, which took place on January 27 1561, would therefore probably not have been rare. Henry Machyn writes of this that there was a sermon and afterwards "goodly singing and playing" and that a number of aldermen were present in their scarlet robes and they gave as a wedding-gift a hundred pairs of gloves. In Stow's time the church seems to have fallen on bad days: for the parishioners then sold a broken bell for half its value rather than go to the expense of recasting it. The strongly Puritan feeling of the City in the mid-seventeenth century is illustrated by the 1641 and 1642 vestry minutes, where orders are given that the picture over the font, the inscriptions on grave-stones "tending to superstition", the crosses set on the walls, the images over the church porch, and even the letters IHS on the silver flagon were all to be removed. After 1666 the parish was united with St Mary le Bow. Its churchyard in Pancras Lane, used as a burial ground until last century, has now been converted into a garden. A City Corporation plaque on its wall commemorates the church site. An iron plaque with the date 1796 and an inscription concerning the right of parishioners to perambulate their boundaries, formerly on railings at the end of the passage beside the garden, has disappeared.

33.   **ST PETER PAUL'S WHARF**

The churchyard of St Peter, Paul's Wharf formed a pleasant oasis in Upper Thames Street until post-war development resulted in its removal. The church was often referred to as St Peter Parva or "Little", to distinguish it from others dedicated to the same saint. In a list of its possessions drawn up about 1180, reference is made to a silver-gilt crucifix containing a relic of the true cross. In 1378 the parish clerk, Thomas Knapet, was committed to Newgate for having spoken disrespectfully of John of Gaunt, Duke of Lancaster. This was one of the few City churches to carry on the Prayer Book services after they had been forbidden under the Cromwellian regime. Evelyn writes on March 25 1649: "I heard Common Prayer (a rare thing in these days) at St Peter's Paul's Wharf, London". For five years, Robert Mossom and others, regardless of danger, used the proscribed services and administered monthly Communions. This brought many of the nobility and gentry to St Peter's and it is said that the galleries where they sat were richly hung with turkey carpets. After 1666 the parish was united with St Benet Paul's Wharf. An old tablet which was recut and set in the wall of the Salvation Army Headquarters in Upper Thames Street, was unfortunately lost during the alterations that occurred in the widening of the street. The only reminder of this small, but interesting church is the modern St Peter's Hill.

34.   **ST PETER WESTCHEAP**

On the corner of Wood Street, Cheapside, stood this church first mentioned in 1196. Stow states that John Shaw, sometime Mayor, who died in 1503, left money for the rebuilding of it with a flat roof and for a steeple. He also says that Thomas Wood, Goldsmith, and Sheriff in 1491, was considered the chief benefactor "because the roof of the middle aisle is supported by images of woodmen". The churchwardens' accounts, which date from 1435, contain items relating to pre-Reformation customs, such as the provision of a room for the morrow-mass priest, the Lenten veil for hanging in the quire, and the expenses incurred in connection with the Palm Sunday ceremonies, particularly bread and wine for the singers of the Passion, and for "setting up the stage for the prophets". In 1559, Elizabeth I was presented with a bible at the church door as she passed through the City. After the Fire the parish was joined to St Matthew, Friday Street. Part of the churchyard still remains. It contains an old plane tree where, in the nineteenth century, four rooks nested. The vestry minutes mention the iron railings as set up in 1712 to replace the then existing wall. These bear a medallion showing St Peter with his keys, and on the reverse side, the date and names of the churchwardens. The small shops fronting on Cheapside were, according to a tablet on the north wall, erected at the sole cost and charges of the parish in 1687.

They are successors to the "Long Shop", originally built here in 1401 and frequently mentioned in the church records. Wordsworth used this corner of Wood Street as the scene for his poem *The Reverie of Poor Susan*.

35.   ST THOMAS THE APOSTLE

The earliest reference to this church occurs near the end of the twelfth century. Stow calls it "a proper church", though the only monuments remaining were some coats of arms either carved in stone or in the windows. Among those buried here was William Littlebury, Mayor in 1487, nicknamed "Horne" by Edward IV, from his excellent horn-blowing. In his will he provided that the four church bells should be replaced, but this does not seem to have been carried out. William Harrison, whose *Description of England* contains a valuable and lively account of Tudor social life, was born in the parish of St Thomas in 1534 and held the benefice between 1583 and 1587 in plurality with his Rectory of Radwinter in Essex. During the 1650s the church became the scene of disorders, since its lecturer or minister, John Rogers, was one of the leading Fifth Monarchy Men. In a letter to Oliver Cromwell in 1653, Rogers spoke of "a solemn humiliation before the Lord". His uncomplimentary references to the Lord Protector on that occasion led to his arrest. The church was destroyed in 1666 and the parish afterwards amalgamated with St Mary Aldermary. Its churchyard remained until the nineteenth century when, on the widening of Queen Street and Cloak Lane, the human remains were reinterred in a stone paved vault on the east side of Queen Street, now removed. The church site is marked by paved ground in front of some fine eighteenth-century residences, now offices. There is a City Corporation plaque on the corner of Great St Thomas Apostle, and also a stone tablet indicating the parish boundaries, with the date 1814 and the names of the two churchwardens — John Cockrill and George Cock.

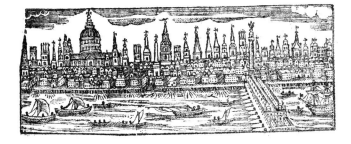

II
Churches Demolished Between the Late Eighteenth Century and 1939

At the heart of the City stood the church of St Christopher le Stocks which was among the earliest of those rebuilt by Wren after the Great Fire. It was also the first to be pulled down when, in 1781, space was required for the extension of the Bank of England. Its demolition ushered in an era during which twenty-seven churches vanished from the "Square Mile". Various factors played a part in their removal: the construction of the new London Bridge and access to it; the serious fire at the Royal Exchange and the rebuilding which followed; and the formation of new thoroughfares like Queen Victoria Street. The glimpse into City churches afforded by Charles Dickens in The Uncommercial Traveller, *where he referred to musty service-books, threadbare pulpit-cushions, and the entire church furniture "in a very advanced stage of exhaustion", did nothing for their image. Again, the tendency to denigrate Wren's architecture in favour of Victorian "Gothick" resulted in so drastic a "restoration" of some City churches that few could argue for their retention. Above all, was the indisputable fact that the City was losing its resident population and becoming a place of day-time workers who departed every evening for homes in the suburbs where new places of worship were increasingly needed. The answer to this need, as certain officials of the London diocese saw it, was to demolish City churches, sell their sites, and with the proceeds build fresh ones outside the capital. The passing of the Union of Benefices Act of 1860 enabled this to be put into practice. So, for example, in due course with their parishes joined to those of remaining City churches, St Dionis Backchurch would become St Dionis Parsons Green and St Peter le Poer Old Broad Street be replaced by St Peter le Poer Friern Barnet. Dr Winnington-Ingram, who was Bishop of London during almost the first forty years of the twentieth century, gave encouragement to this policy and in his time some half-a-dozen City churches disappeared, the last being All Hallows Lombard Street in 1939. By then, however, the City was faced with an even greater threat.*

36. ALL HALLOWS BREAD STREET

"A proper church" is Stow's description of All Hallows Bread Street which was first mentioned in the thirteenth century. Following a quarrel between two priests leading to bloodshed, the church was closed for a month during the time of Henry VIII. Laurence Saunders, who was Rector in Mary's reign, was burned at the stake for preaching Protestant doctrine. In 1559 during a thunderstorm, the spire of All Hallows was struck by lightning and part of it fell into the street, killing a dog and throwing to the ground a man who was playing with the animal. The outstanding event in the church's history occurred on 20 December 1608 when, according to the parish registers now in Guildhall Library, there was "baptized John the sonne of John Milton, Scrivener". The parish clerk, who himself later succumbed to the Great Plague, entered in the register of 1665 the fact that certain parishioners who then died were buried in the Quakers' ground — a unique entry in the City's parochial records. Destroyed in the Great Fire, All Hallows was rebuilt by Wren who provided a fine tower with an arcaded upper storey surmounted by four pinnacles. Hatton, in 1708, says: "There is no table of benefactors, nor any worth it as the churchwarden (who is a hosier) expressed himself to me. But I hope 'tis only a modest temper they have to conceal their charity". Hatton mentions too the finely-carved pulpit enriched with cherubs which is now at St Vedast Foster Lane. All Hallows was demolished in 1876 to make way for warehouses, the parish being united with that of St Mary le Bow. Part of the proceeds from the sale of the site was used to build the church of All Hallows East India Dock Road. A stone tablet bearing the head of John Milton which used to

mark where All Hallows formerly stood on the corner of Bread Street and Watling Street was destroyed in World War II, but a plaque recording his baptism can be seen on the west wall of St Mary's facing Bow Churchyard. There are also parish boundary marks in Watling Street and Court.

G. Druce Delin. Alhallows Breadstreet T. Bowles Sculp

37.   **ALL HALLOWS THE GREAT**

Situated beside the Steelyard where the merchants of the Hanseatic League
had their headquarters in medieval London, All Hallows and its parish must then
have been flourishing. It was known as "the Great" to distinguish it from its neigh-
bour All Hallows the Less and, according to Stow, was also called "ad foenum in the
Ropery" because hay was sold at the nearby Hay Wharf and ropes were made and sold
in the high street. Stow also refers to a cloister on the south side of the churchyard
where burials were still taking place in the late sixteenth century, even though this had
become in a ruinous condition. Pepys notes in his *Diary* that certain of the parishioners were so keen to welcome back Charles II that they set up the Royal arms private-
ly more than a month before the Restoration. At the same time, as the vestry minutes
of December 1660 reveal, this did not prevent them from delivering a petition to the
Archbishop that Robert Bragge, a Commonwealth intruder who had served them for
eight years and was "sound in doctrine and of a holy conversation", might be allowed
to continue as their minister. The "seamy" side of a riverside parish is illustrated by an
entry in the churchwardens' accounts of 1663–64 to the effect that 8s.8d. was spent
on burying someone "that cut his own throat". While the combustible material such
as oil and tar which proliferated on its wharves ensured the destruction of the church
in the Great Fire. Wren rebuilt All Hallows the Great, but according to Malcolm in his
Londinium Redivivum, because of the church's confined situation, he took no pains in
designing the outside which was "as plain and as dirty as can be". Malcolm further
revealed that the cart-wheels almost touched the north side of the church in Thames
Street; hence it is not surprising that the tower was removed in 1876 to widen the

street. In 1894 the rest of the building was demolished, and the parish united with that of St Michael Paternoster Royal. Part of the money from the sale of the site was used to build All Hallows Gospel Oak in north London. A portion of All Hallows' churchyard and a small rebuilt brick tower on the west side remained until after World War II, when they were destroyed to make way for what is now the City Fire Station. The chancel screen with its fine carving, including that of an eagle, which had been presented to All Hallows in the seventeenth century by a rich merchant, Theodore Jacobson, in memory of the close associations between the church and the Hanseatic League in bygone days, can be seen in St Margaret's Lothbury. Also from the former All Hallows are statues of Moses and Aaron which now adorn the east end of St Michael Paternoster Royal and a carved figure of Charity attached to the lectern there. A building on the south side of Upper Thames Street bears on its wall a parish boundary mark, dated 1817.

38.   ALL HALLOWS LOMBARD STREET

Shortly before the outbreak of World War II, a small group paid a visit to All Hallows Lombard Street where a University of London Extra-Mural Lecturer expounded on the church's history and furnishings, especially the splendid wood-work with curtains so delicately carved that, as he remarked, one felt like drawing them aside. Within five years of that afternoon, All Hallows had been condemned as a dangerous structure; a closing service had taken place and what had for long been known as the "hidden" or "invisible" church — so hemmed in was it by office build-ings — was being reconstructed on the Chertsey Road at Twickenham. The rebuilt All Hallows with its tall white campanile — now far better seen than it had ever been in the City — and with a narthex and cloister containing monuments from its predecessor as well as what, until 1865, had been the entrance gateway, were all in place for the consecration service held in November 1940. All Hallows Lombard Street was among the few churches which could claim to date from Saxon times, since it was first men-tioned in 1054 when given to Christchurch Canterbury. Stow says that the street in which it stood was "far broader than now it is, being straitened by encroachments". He adds that towards the end of the fifteenth century the church was newly built, the main part being completed in 1516 and the bell-tower in 1544. If Wren was slow in getting down to its rebuilding after the Fire, he and his colleagues more than com-pensated for the delay in the work which they carried out. So Hatton, in his *New View* of 1708, could say: "The altarpiece is the most spacious and best-carved that I have thus far met with" and he mentioned particularly the Pelican nourishing her young, the seven candlesticks representing those of the churches in the New Testament book *Revelation* and the figures of Time and Death above the door-cases. Malcolm, a century later, described the parish as "a mere chain of courts and alleys" and referred to the Rector's house as in "a situation totally unfit for a respectable tenant". Many people no doubt remember All Hallows for an event recorded in John Wesley's *Journal*. Wesley was ascending the pulpit-stairs when he discovered he had come without a sermon. Mentioning this to a woman nearby, he received the reply: "Cannot you trust God?" Such was the effect on him that he never again preached from a written sermon. The site of All Hallows is now occupied by Barclays Bank, and the former parish united with that of the nearby St Edmund the King. There are boundary marks in Gracechurch Street and Lombard Street and Court. But it is to Twickenham that one should go, for there can be seen the many treasures transferred from the City — not least those curtains so exquisitely fashioned by an unknown seventeenth-century wood-carver.

39. **ALL HALLOWS STAINING**

Named "Staining", says Stow, because All Hallows was built of stone when most other City churches were of timber, or, according to modern authorities, from an early connection with Staines in Middlesex, its tower certainly seems to have a charmed life. Built in the fifteenth century, it still stands in Mark Lane and Star Alley as a reminder of how many of the pre-Fire churches must have appeared. Stow also draws attention to the wanton destruction of monuments that occurred during the sixteenth-century religious upheavals, when he writes of one benefactor: "His name remaineth painted in the church roof: if it had been in brass, it would not have remained there so long." When Princess Elizabeth was released from imprisonment in the Tower during the reign of her sister Mary Tudor, she attended a service of thanksgiving at All Hallows, and later as Queen presented the church with a set of silk bell ropes. One of these may have been pulled by the ringers when, on 9 February 1586/87, they were paid a shilling for ringing for "joye of ye execution of ye Queen of Scots". The church escaped the Great Fire, but, except for the tower, fell down in 1671. It was subsequently rebuilt, though not by Wren. All Hallows was one of the four London churches where, in 1688, James II's Declaration of Indulgence was read. The officiating minister was, in Macaulay's words, "a wretch named Timothy Hall" and the congregation immediately got up and walked out. In 1870 the body of the church was finally demolished, although again the tower was spared, the parish being united with that of St Olave Hart Street. Communion plate and furnishings went to All

Hallows Bromley-by-Bow which was built with money from the sale of the site. A bell dated 1458 — the oldest in the City — is in Grocers' Hall, and though this was severely damaged in a fire which destroyed the Hall in 1967, it has since been restored. Beneath the tower of All Hallows is a Norman crypt brought here in 1873 from the former Lambe's Chapel in Monkwell Street by the Clothworkers' Company. This Company cares for the surrounding churchyard and has also provided the modern parish hall in Mark Lane. Two sword-rests from All Hallows Staining can be seen in the church of St Olave, as well as a stained-glass window depicting the Princess Elizabeth's visit. Parish boundary marks are in Billiter Street and Fenchurch Avenue, but a boundary stone of 1725 which, until a few years ago, stood on the pavement in London Street, has now gone.

40. **HOLY TRINITY GOUGH SQUARE**

The generosity of some of the Livery Companies to the Church in the City deserves to be recorded. For example, that of the Worshipful Company of Goldsmiths has been shown in its post-war gifts to St Paul's Cathedral. Similarly, when in the 1830s the parish of St Bride Fleet Street felt the need of additional accommodation for those attending Sunday worship, the Goldsmiths' Company came to its aid by donating a site from the property it owned in the neighbourhood of Gough Square in order that a church could be built to serve that part of the parish. It further contributed the sum of £500 for the purpose of endowment. So, on 23 June 1838, there was consecrated by the Bishop of London the church of Holy Trinity, Pemberton Row, Gough Square. From a sermon preached the following day by the Reverend Thomas Dale, Vicar of St Bride's, on the text: "The Spirit of the Lord is upon me, because he hath anointed me to preach the gospel to the poor", coupled with the fact that of the 1100 sittings the free and cheaper ones were fully occupied, it seems that Holy Trinity was built specially for the poorer inhabitants of St Bride's parish. Designed by John Shaw and hexagonal in shape, the building itself was, by all accounts, of inferior quality. At the same time, the vestry minutes, covering the years from 1845 to 1906 and in Guildhall Library, indicate that during its comparatively short life it was served by a number of faithful churchwardens and others. Indeed, the efforts of one churchwarden to restore and beautify the church in 1891 were commended by the vestry. By 1905, however, a Commission appointed by the then Bishop of London, Dr Winnington-Ingram, unanimously recommended that the parishes of Holy Trinity and St Bride should once more be united. At a special vestry meeting held on 8 March 1906 it was agreed that St Bride's should become the church of the united parishes and that Holy Trinity — in the words of *The City Press* of two days later "not an historic or even a beautiful edifice" and "the raison d'être of which had long ceased to exist" — should be pulled down and the site and materials disposed of by the Ecclesiastical Commissioners. According to *The London Encyclopaedia*, "Trinity Church Passage, Fetter Lane commemorates the church"; but this was built over in the early 1980s and no longer exists. Still, those who glance up at the walls of a building in Pemberton Row will see property marks, bearing leopards' heads and covered cups — part of the arms of a Livery Company of whose liberality they are a reminder.

41. **ST ALPHAGE LONDON WALL**

News of the murder of the Archbishop of Canterbury, Alphage, by the Danes in 1012 shocked the people of England, so that when later that century a church was built beside London Wall, it was natural that it should be dedicated to the saint's memory. Its churchyard, backed by a section of the Wall and containing possibly a few stones from the original St Alphage church, remains today as a garden. By the sixteenth century the church itself was on the point of collapse. It so happened that the nearby Elsyng Spital, founded by a wealthy Mercer William Elsyng a couple of centuries earlier to provide a home for a hundred blind men, had suffered in the dissolution of the religious houses under Henry VIII. This then became a place of worship for the congregation of St Alphage. The inhumane treatment meted out by Henry VIII to the blind inhabitants of Prior Elsyng's hospice was almost matched by the religious intolerance revealed in the 1559 parish records. On two separate occasions that year the churchwardens of St Alphage were granted payment. First:

> "for our breakefast that day that we dyd serch a bought the parishe for pyctures and images that were paynted", and second:

> "for our brekefast that day that we dyd ascemble to gether for to know whether there were any anabaptyste in the parish dwellying or no".

The church escaped the Great Fire with only slight damage. However, by 1777 much of it had to be rebuilt, though the ancient tower was left standing. Despite the fact that additions were made to the building early in the twentieth century, the church of St Alphage was clearly no longer needed and in 1924 the parish was united with that of St Mary Aldermanbury to which many of the fittings and furnishings were transferred. Once again, the old tower was spared — as it was during the bombing in World War II which devastated so much of this neighbourhood. Now restored, it stands on the north side of London Wall, almost opposite the hall of the Brewers' Company. Anyone who is interested enough to venture to cross the road to see it, surely deserves to be rewarded with the sight of a board, bearing a note as to what is certainly among the City's most miraculous survivals.

42.   **ST ANTHOLIN BUDGE ROW**

Of all the City churches demolished in the nineteenth century, the loss of St Antholin's seems to have caused the greatest regret. Despite strong efforts to ensure that at least the tower with its octagonal spire should be preserved as a memorial, traffic considerations proved even stronger and in 1875 St Antholin's was demolished to make way for the new Queen Victoria Street, the parish being united with that of St Mary Aldermary. The pre-Fire church dedicated to St Anthony of Padua — the letter 'l' appears to have crept into the name by mistake — is first mentioned in the early 1100s. Henry Colet, a Mercer and Mayor, was among medieval benefactors and his son John, the founder of St Paul's School and Dean of the Cathedral, was born in the parish. St Antholin's became famous during the reign of Elizabeth I as a stronghold of Puritanism and lectures "after Geneva fashion" were regularly delivered there at five o'clock in the morning. There are numerous literary references to these lectures, as when, for example, Sir William Davenant refers to "two disciples of St Tantlin that rise to long exercise before day". Even after the demolition of the church, the St Antholin Lectures continued to be held until well into the middle of the twentieth century at St Mary Aldermary and other City churches — although at a more civilised hour! Destroyed in the Great Fire, St Antholin's was rebuilt by Wren in 1682, being constructed on an irregular site and having an oval-shaped dome on eight columns. In the eighteenth century John Wesley preached there on several occasions, noting in his

Journal on 15 November 1778 that "the people were so wedged together that it was with difficulty I got in". Part of the money from the sale of St Antholin's site was used to build St Anthony's Nunhead, and to this the reredos from the City church went. Prior to World War II there was a small open space on the corner of Budge Row and Sise Lane, containing a stone tablet on which was engraved a picture of the former church's exterior. Except for this tablet which, though slightly damaged, is preserved in the north vestibule of St Mary Aldermary, all has gone, the site now being occupied by Bucklersbury House. However, a portion of the stone spire can be found at Round Hill, Forest Hill in South London. To it is affixed the following inscription:

"This Tower is the Upper Part of the Spire of the Church of St Antholin, Watling Street, one of Sir Christopher Wren's City Churches built between 1678 and 1688. After the demolition of the Church in 1875 the Tower was moved to his garden at Round Hill House by the Owner, Robert Harrild".

Sydenham Society, 1987.

43.   **ST BARTHOLOMEW BY THE EXCHANGE**
Situated at the south-east corner of Bartholomew Lane, this church, first mentioned in the early thirteenth century, was, according to Stow, rebuilt by an alderman assisted by one of the Sheriffs. This gives an indication as to the status of many of those who worshipped at St Bartholomew's and the fact that it was always a rich parish. The sixteenth-century Reformer, Miles Coverdale, Bishop of Exeter and one of the translators of the English Bible, was buried in St Bartholomew's in 1569, but after its destruction in the nineteenth century his remains were transferred to St Magnus, of which he was sometime Rector. Stow mentions that a Sheriff who died in 1499 left money for a sermon to be preached at the church every Good Friday from 6 until 8 in the morning on the subject of Christ's Passion. Later benefactors endowed various lectureships there, so that those attending St Bartholomew's must have had a surfeit of godly instruction. One of those benefactors who played an active part in the church's life during the early seventeenth century was Richard Fishborne, a wealthy Mercer, whose tomb can be seen in the ambulatory of his Company's Hall in Ironmonger Lane. The vestry minutes refer to "the sadd and dreadfull" Fire of 1666 which severely damaged the church. Wren completed its rebuilding in 1679, but the curious tower which is clearly visible in early nineteenth-century prints, has an unfinished appearance. This has led some to believe that Wren either kept the original tower or produced a replica of it. An article in the *Gentleman's Magazine* of 1840 describes the interior of St Bartholomew's as "light and graceful" and notes the excellent quality of its furnishings. When in 1841 the rebuilding of the Royal Exchange, after a disastrous fire, necessitated the demolition of the church, these furnishings were carefully preserved in order to be installed some years later in the new church of St Bartholomew Moor Lane, built by C.R. Cockerell. This in turn was demolished in 1902 to allow for the extension of the Metropolitan Railway, and the pulpit and sounding-board, as well as the font and cover, then went to St Bartholomew's Craven Hill, Tottenham. In the City itself there can be seen at St Vedast Foster Lane the organ

originally constructed by Harris and Byfield for use at St Bartholomew by the Exchange. Having in 1841 gone to Moor Lane and then early this century to a church in Fulham, it is now in its fourth home where, after Noel Mander's restoration of it to pristine condition, it looks as splendid as when it was first built in 1731. A City Corporation plaque marks the site of St Bartholomew's church, the removal of which was, according to the *Gentleman's Magazine* of 1840, treated with apathy.

44.   **ST BENET FINK**

Situated between Cornhill and Threadneedle Street, Finch Lane was so called from the Finke family who resided there. One of its members, Robert Finke, rebuilt the nearby church of St Benet which was named after him but destroyed in the Great Fire. The plan of the Wren church, begun in 1670, was described in the *Gentleman's Magazine* as "uncommon and very effective". The external walls formed a decagon, at the west end of which was a square stone tower surmounted by a dome and small cupola. The adornment of the interior owed much to the gift of £1000 from George Holman — an instance of generosity all the more remarkable since the donor was a Roman Catholic. Hatton says that Holman would have given the parishioners an organ as well, had they not refused it. Some said this was because of the expense involved in keeping it in repair and maintaining an organist, but according to others "owing to their want of esteem for the melodious harmony which that instrument provides in a congregation". Nevertheless, as a token of their gratitude they presented Holman with two pews and a vault to him and his heirs for ever. The parish registers of April 1673 record the burial of Thomas Sharrow, late churchwarden, who was killed by an accidental fall in a vault near Paternoster Row and, as was supposed, had lain there eleven days and nights before he was found; to which entry are added the words: "Let all that read this take heed of drink"! On 9 April 1801, there took place in St Benet's the baptism of John Henry Newman, who was born in a house in Old Broad Street almost opposite the church and who later became a Cardinal — yet another link with the Roman Catholic Church. The fire which destroyed the Royal Exchange in the winter of 1838 also heralded the end of St Benet Fink: for in the replanning and rebuilding which followed it was decided that the church should be demolished. This took place in 1844, the parish being united with that of St Peter le Poer. From part of the proceeds of the sale, a new church of St Benet Fink was erected in Tottenham and later, following the closure of St Peter's, this received some Communion plate from its City predecessor. The disposal of the furniture of St Benet's at a public auction proved a fiasco, with items such as the pulpit, sounding-board and stairs going for only £15.5s.0d. A City Corporation plaque can be seen on the wall of a building in Royal Exchange Avenue. Paintings of Moses and Aaron which were formerly part of the altarpiece of St Benet's are now in Emmanuel School, Wandsworth, London. (See: Paul Hetherington, "The altarpiece for Wren's church of St Benet Fink", *Apollo*, July 1995, pp.44-46).

45.   **ST BENET GRACECHURCH**

Situated on the corner of Gracechurch and Fenchurch Streets, this was, according to Stow, called "Grass Church", from the herb market which used to be held opposite its west door. We learn from the sixteenth-century churchwardens' accounts that 3s.4d. was paid to a plasterer at the beginning of the reign of Mary Tudor to remove the Biblical texts which had been set up on the walls of the interior during the time of her Protestant brother Edward VI. Later records contain the name of Grace Church, a foundling for whose upbringing the parish was responsible. Destroyed in the Great Fire, the church as rebuilt by Wren in 1685 was, although spacious, not one of the architect's best. Nevertheless, there exists an attractive engraving which depicts St Benet's beside the roadway leading to old London Bridge. A most curious item is to be found in the churchwardens' accounts during the 1690s when, for several years, the sexton was paid sixpence "for ringing the pancake bell" — presumably to usher in the customary Shrove Tuesday festivities. In 1791 Dr George Gaskin exchanged his country benefice for that of St Benet Gracechurch to enable him to fulfil more easily his duties as secretary of the Society for Promoting Christian Knowledge, to which he was then appointed. Thomas Broughton, his father-in-law and a previous SPCK secretary, had been Rector of All Hallows Lombard Street just across the road. The portraits of both men are in the Society's London headquarters at Marylebone and provide illustrations of the dress and appearance of City clergy in the eighteenth century. In 1867 St Benet's was demolished for road-widening, the parish being united with that of All Hallows nearby. Its removal, said *The Times* of 25 October that year, "will greatly facilitate the traffic in that part of the City". Money from the sale of the site helped to build St Benet Mile End Road. As this church did not want the finely-carved seventeenth-century pulpit, it was purchased by the then Rector of St Olave Hart Street where, restored and on a different base, it can still be seen. Other reminders of St Benet Gracechurch are a City Corporation plaque denoting the site, boundary marks in Gracechurch Street and Lombard Court, and the passage-way known as St Benet's Place.

46.   **ST CHRISTOPHER LE STOCKS**

The distinctive title borne by this church came from the nearby Stocks Market which, in bygone days, occupied the site of the present Mansion House. Hatton, writing in 1708, says that he had seen engraved on a small plate over the Vestry door the following: "this church of St Christovil was finished in the year of our Lord 1462, as was found by an old monument in a glass window of this vestry 1592". According to Stow, the steeple was newly built at the beginning of the sixteenth century and in 1621 was repaired and beautified at the charge of the parish. In 1624, a benefactor left £20 a year to be given to the curate, on condition that he read divine service in the church at 6 o'clock in the morning every day in the week for ever. Although St Christopher's suffered severe damage in the Great Fire, Wren was able to use much of the surviving material in his rebuilding of 1671, and after further repair and beautifying in 1696, Newcourt was moved to say that it "is now as fair a church as ever". Nevertheless, unforeseen events led to its becoming the first of Wren's City churches to be pulled down. Faced by the Gordon Rioters of 1780, the Directors of the Bank of England, who had then gained possession of almost all the parish, were concerned by the possibility of similar groups occupying St Christopher's church, while moreover, they were at the same time anxious to enlarge the Bank. Hence, in 1781, the church was sacrificed, although its churchyard was allowed to remain for many years to come. W.G. Bell, in *The Great Fire of London*, says the last person to be buried there was a bank clerk named Jenkins who, because he was more than seven feet tall, feared that after his death his body would be dug up and sold for medical research and welcomed the security provided by a churchyard within the Bank itself. Following the church's demolition, the parish was united with that of St Margaret Lothbury, where several treasures originally in St Christopher's can be seen. These include the paintings of Moses and Aaron on the East wall and a bronze head of Peter le Maire, the work of Hubert le Sueur, who made the equestrian statue of Charles I at Charing Cross. During the rebuilding of the Bank of England in 1934, a fine incised Purbeck marble gravestone of the early fourteenth century was discovered. It shows a man, in tunic and hood, with long curly hair — probably a City merchant. The slab is now displayed in the Victoria and Albert Museum. The former reredos, which was for a long time at Great Burstead, Essex, now forms the magnificent altarpiece in St Vedast Foster Lane. There are parish boundary marks in Princes Street and Threadneedle Street.

47.   **ST DIONIS BACKCHURCH**

This church, which stood at the corner of Fenchurch Street and Lime Street, was the only one in the City to be dedicated to the patron saint of France — possibly a reflection of the strong French influence which prevailed in England during the thirteenth century, when St Dionis is first mentioned. The title "Backchurch" is generally explained as a reference to the fact that the church lay back from the street and behind a row of houses and shops, as may be seen from old engravings. It also distinguishes it from the church of St Gabriel Fen which, until 1666, stood in the middle of Fenchurch Street and was frequently referred to as "Forechurch". Pepys in his *Diary* says that he visited St Dionis on Christmas Day 1664 and noted the "very great store of fine women there is in this church, more than I know anywhere else about us". Burnt in the Great Fire, it was among the first churches to be rebuilt by Wren, the main part being completed by 1674, though the steeple was not added until ten years later. Hatton, writing in 1708, includes a list of benefactors and of their various gifts to the Wren church. This was demolished in 1878, the parish then being united with that of All Hallows Lombard Street. The proceeds from the sale of the site went towards the building of St Dionis Parsons Green, where the Communion-table, pulpit and font formerly in the City church are still in use. From St Dionis Backchurch came the Stuart Royal Arms and some organ casing in St Edmund Lombard Street. Malcolm, in his *Londinium Redivivum,* mentions that in the parish vestry room several brass syringes, or "squirts", used formerly for extinguishing fires, were to be seen. One of these is now in the Museum of London, having been removed there from St Dionis Hall in Lime Street when this disappeared in the post-war redevelopment of the area. Malcolm also tells of a terrible accident that occurred in the church in November 1803, when the sexton was struck on the head by part of a branch candlestick as it was being taken down and died shortly afterwards. A City Corporation plaque which marked the site of St Dionis is no longer in place, but there remains in Brabant Court a fire-plug inscribed "I. Taylor St DIO BC 1842".

48.   ST GEORGE BOTOLPH LANE

This church, which is first mentioned in the reign of Henry III and the only one in the City to be dedicated to England's patron saint, stood on the west side of Botolph Lane. In contrast to what he found in many churches in his time, Stow could say of St George's that its monuments were "well preserved from spoil". Destroyed in the Great Fire, the church was rebuilt by Wren, allegedly out of the rubble of Old St Paul's. Hatton refers to it in 1708 as "a pretty though small church built of stone". Among its memorials was a tablet to Isaac Milner who died in 1713. A sword-rest to William Beckford, Alderman of Billingsgate Ward, now in St Mary at Hill, bears the inscription: "Sacred to the memory of that real patriot the Right Hon. William Beckford, twice Lord Mayor of London: whose incessant spirited efforts to serve his country hastened his dissolution on the 21 June 1770, in the time of his mayoralty and the 62nd year of his age". The proximity of St George's to Billingsgate Fish Market caused Malcolm, writing of the parish in his *Londinium Redivivum,* to declare: "The narrow streets and alleys and their wet slippery footways will not bear description or invite unnecessary visits". By the latter part of the nineteenth century the condition of St George's had so deteriorated as to cause a scandal. A letter to *The Times* of May 1900 revealed that it was several years since it was "condemned as structurally unsafe and nearly a quarter of a century since the accumulation of human remains in the vaults attracted the notice of the sanitary authorities"; while the writer of another letter of February 1901 stated that the church had been closed to the public for no less a period than ten years, and that during the past thirty years there had been various statements to the effect that the building was either "doomed" or "under sentence of death". The end came in 1904 when St George's was demolished and the parish united with that of St Mary at Hill. Two carved seventeenth-century chairs are now in the nearby church of St Margaret Pattens. The site of the former church is indicated by St George's Lane and there is a parish boundary mark in Botolph Alley.

49.   **ST JAMES DUKE'S PLACE**

A ghostly air seems to pervade that part of the City bounded by Leadenhall Street, Bevis Marks and Creechurch Lane, which is hardly surprising when one recalls the strong religious associations of its past, as well as the fact that one of Jack the Ripper's victims met her death in Mitre Square. Before the dissolution of the monasteries, the area was occupied by the wealthy Priory of Holy Trinity or Christchurch, of which all that is left is a single arch in Swiss Re House on the corner of Leadenhall and Mitre Streets. Following the disposal of the Priory's property, those who settled in what was named Duke's Place, after its new owner the Duke of Norfolk, sought a place of worship and finding St Katherine Cree uncongenial, asked permission of James I to build a church of their own. Consecrated in 1622, this was called St James in the king's honour; as John Strype has it in his edition of Stow's *Survey*:

> "This sacred structure which this senate fames
> Our King has styled the temple of St James".

It appears that when the Lord Mayor and Sheriffs were made aware of the royal approval, they wished to share in the glory, and so actively supported the building of the church. Malcolm, in his *Londinium Redivivum*, says that the Lord Mayor, Edward Barkham, "glazed the East window in which he inserted his arms, and an inscription informing the world of his liberality"! The church escaped the Great Fire, but by the early years of the eighteenth century had fallen into so ruinous a condition that the parishioners were forced to rebuild it. Because the parish was small and chiefly inhabited by poor folk, an appeal was issued in the *Post Boy* of 5 December 1727 begging for financial assistance, otherwise "the work must fall short of that decency which were to be wished for". As it was, the building that arose is described as "a plain warehouse-like erection of brick". The tower appears to have contained stonework, not merely from the 1622 church, but belonging to the original Priory buildings. Since the patronage of St James was held by the City Corporation, claims were made in the late seventeenth century that marriages could be performed there without a licence and the church became notorious for the number of such irregular weddings, until the practice was ended by Act of Parliament. The population of the area became increasingly Jewish during the nineteenth century, so that St James's was no longer needed. Hence in the 1870s the parish was united with St Katharine Cree, to which the monuments, mural tablets and fittings were transferred. A note in *The Times* of 15 August 1874 records that on the previous day the demolition of St James's church and the removal of bodies, filling more than 180 chests, had been completed. A City Corporation plaque formerly marking the church site in Mitre Square has gone, but there is a parish boundary mark in Creechurch Lane, while St James's Passage and Duke's Place are other reminders of the past.

50.   ST KATHERINE COLEMAN

On the south side of Fenchurch Street, not far from where is now the Station, there stood until 1926 the church of St Katherine Coleman. According to Stow, its distinctive name was "taken of a great Haw yard, or Garden, of old time called Coleman haw". First mentioned in the fourteenth century, St Katherine's south aisle was restored or repaired in 1489 by William White, Draper and Mayor. In 1624 a vestry was built and "a gallery was made for the poor of the parish to sit in". Some people associated with the church in the seventeenth century had strong Stuart sympathies. Thus, Henry Kilberd, who was appointed by Laud as Rector in 1641, was ejected during the Cromwellian regime for his loyalty to the King; while Hatton, in 1708, speaks of there being in St Katherine's a portrait of Charles I in his royal robes and at his devotions. He also mentions a monument to the wife of Sir Richard Heigham, "one of the Gentleman Pensioners in ordinary attendance to our sovereign Lord King Charles" and another to Robert Thatcher, a servant "to our royal King Charles when he was prince". The church narrowly escaped the Great Fire, but was rebuilt in the 1730s by James Horne, an architect and surveyor responsible for a number of churches in a style described as "vernacular Palladian". Although at the time of its closure St Katherine's was said to have "no beauty of form or decoration", it was not without friends: for, as *The City Press* of 26 November 1921 reported, the final service on the previous Sunday was most inspiring, the church being absolutely crowded, with a small orchestra assisting, and the sermon being delivered by the Rector of St Olave Hart Street, with which the parish was to be united. In a modern window in the Lady Chapel of St Olave, St Katherine is depicted. From the money obtained by the sale of the site, a new church dedicated to St Katherine Coleman was built at Westway, on a housing estate close to Hammersmith. Unfortunately, this building together with the furnishings it contained, many of them transferred there from the former City church, suffered severe bomb damage during World War II. Part of the old churchyard of St Katherine Coleman, with railings and stone pillars, remains in St Katherine's Row off Fenchurch Street and a City Corporation plaque indicates its site. There are parish boundary marks in Northumberland Alley and London Street.

51. ST MARTIN OUTWICH

Until the 1870s, the magnificent alabaster effigies of Sir John de Oteswich and his wife, dating from about 1400 and now in St Helen's Bishopsgate, were to be seen in the church of St Martin Outwich which, as a City Corporation plaque records, then stood on the corner of Threadneedle Street and Bishopsgate. Dedicated to St Martin, it took its distinctive name of "Outwich" from the fact that it owed much to the benefactions of Sir John and other members of the Oteswich family. In later documents it is referred to as St Martin "at the well with two buckets" from, according to Stow, its proximity to "a fair well with two buckets so fastened that the drawing up of the one let down the other, but of late that well is turned into a pump". Due to lack of space the parishioners were buried in ground near St Paul's Cathedral until, in 1539, they acquired their own cemetery — as is recorded in the churchwardens' accounts: "To the Masters of Pappe for the purchase of the churchyard £2.13s.4d.". This referred to a piece of ground in London Wall close to what had been a hospital for aged and infirm priests, known as "The Papey". St Martin escaped the flames of 1666, but almost a century later, on 7 November 1765, the church was severely damaged by a fire which broke out in a wig-maker's shop in Bishopsgate Street and quickly spread. Fortunately, the marble font adorned with cherubs, mentioned by Hatton in 1708, and the pulpit that he described as "pretty considering 'tis of an antique mode" were spared. Despite the repairs then carried out, which included the construction of a new steeple, it was decided in 1794 that St Martin's should be pulled down and rebuilt, though on a reduced site, necessitating the unusual form of an oval. The architect employed was Samuel P. Cockerell, who saw it as his finest work and sent some of the designs to the Royal Academy. Others however, were more critical, one writer, W.F. Loftie, declaring that it looked more like a gaol than a church. At the consecration service in 1798 the beadle must have appeared resplendent in his laced uniform and hat and bearing a staff with silver top — all donated for the occasion. However, the omens for the future were not good. Malcolm, in his *Londinium Redivivum* of 1807, commented on the deterioration already taking place in distemper painting on the east wall, where rays emanating from the Saviour's brow were falling off, and the knee of an angel had expanded into a huge tumour. Then, in the *Gentleman's Magazine* of July 1808, there appeared a note that St Martin's had been robbed of all its plate.

Perhaps, therefore, it was not so surprising that *The Times* of September 1873 should report that preliminary steps had been taken for the removal from the seventy-five year old church of tablets and monuments to St Helen's, which thenceforth became that of the united parishes.

52. ST MARY SOMERSET

Before the widening and development of Upper Thames Street in the 1970s, a visitor to the tower of the former church of St Mary Somerset might still have been able to imagine the time when there existed a nearby wharf called "Summers Hithe". From this the church perhaps derived its distinctive name, later corrupted to "Somerset". And as one gazed on the then surviving churchyard, it was still possible to picture the gathering together of the fourteenth-century weavers of Brabant, who in 1370 were ordered by the Mayor to meet there, following disturbances with their Flemish rivals who assembled in the churchyard of St Laurence Pountney. The church itself, which was first mentioned in a late twelfth-century deed, was destroyed in the Great Fire. It was rebuilt by Wren and completed in 1695. A century later, Malcolm in his *Londinium Redivivum* indicates the attitude of many of his contemporaries towards the Methodists, when in his account of St Mary Somerset he writes: "When I mention that the late well-known Methodist Mr Gunn was a preacher in it on certain days, the trampled and dirty state of the church will not be wondered at"! In the autumn of 1805 the Communion plate was stolen and, despite efforts, the thief was never traced, so that a new set had to be purchased. Sixty years later, the old church — described as being "dingy, dull and empty" — was no longer required; and so it was scheduled for demolition, the parish being united with that of St Nicholas Cole Abbey. According to *The City Press* report, the final service took place on Friday 1 February 1867 with about seventy people present, not including the children of Queenhithe Ward Schools. From the proceeds of the sale of the site the church of St Mary Britannia

Street, Hoxton, was built, and to this went the altar, font, pulpit and bell. Happily, the square stone tower of St Mary Somerset was recognised as being among the finest examples of Wren's work, and was spared under the Union of City Benefices Act. During the years between the two World Wars it served as a quiet place where women workers in the City could find rest and refreshment. Now, firmly locked, the old tower — which, according to the inscription it bears, was restored by the City Corporation in 1956 — appears rather lonely, despite the efforts of a small patch of grass with flowers and trees below to brighten it.

53. ST MARY MAGDALEN OLD FISH STREET

"A small church, having but few monuments" is all that Stow has to say of St Mary Magdalen, first mentioned in 1181. Situated in the eastern part of Knightrider Street, then known as Old Fish Street from what was the City's oldest retail fish market, its parishioners would, no doubt, have witnessed some lively scenes in medieval days. During the persecution of the Anglican Church under Cromwell in the mid-seventeenth century, John Evelyn records in his *Diary* that on Easter Day 1653, he and his family were able to receive Holy Communion at St Mary Magdalen's "where a Scotchman preached on the Gospel". Destroyed in the Great Fire, the church was rebuilt by Wren in 1685, having above its tower a unique stone lantern on five steps. The Reverend R.H. Barham, author of *The Ingoldsby Legends*, was Rector from 1824 to 1842 and was later buried in the church. According to *The City Press* report, a serious fire broke out in a warehouse in Knightrider Street on the morning of 2 December 1886. The flames quickly spread and attacked the roof of St Mary Magdalen's nearby, leaving the building in a ruined state. After this the church was pulled down and the parish united with that of St Martin Ludgate. Old Change and Knightrider Street, where St Mary Magdalen formerly stood, have been so drastically altered in post-war redevelopment that it is no longer possible to locate its site, the City Corporation plaque which previously marked it having been removed. There are, however, some survivals now at St Martin's. They include a painting by R. Browne of the Ascension, which was formerly above the altar-piece in St Mary Magdalen's, and monuments in the vestibule. Most precious is a small brass plate which depicts a benefactor, believed to be Thomas Berrie, a merchant of the Staple, with the date 1586 above him. It bears an inscription with typically Elizabethan sentiments, and ending with the lines:

> "How smale soever the gifte shall be,
> Thanke God for him who gave it thee.
> xii penie loves to xii poore foulkes
> Geve everie sabothe day for aye".

There is an identical brass plaque at Walton-on-the-Hill in Lancashire, to which Thomas Berrie made a similar benefaction.

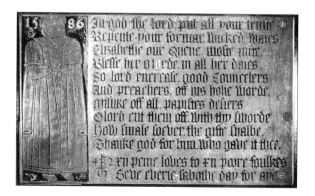

54. ST MATTHEW FRIDAY STREET

Situated in a part of Friday Street between Cheapside and Watling Street which was built over in the post-War reconstruction of the City, the church of St Matthew is first mentioned in the time of Henry III. According to Stow, Friday Street was so called because of the fishmongers dwelling there and serving Friday's market; but, surprisingly, the names of none are to be found in the parish records. A notable worshipper at St Matthew's during the reign of James I was Sir Hugh Myddleton, who brought the New River to London. He officiated as churchwarden and, when he died in 1631, was buried in the pre-Fire church. During the nineteenth century, following the church's demolition, an unsuccessful attempt was made to locate Myddleton's coffin and monument. St Matthew's became a centre of religious controversy in the seventeenth century when the Puritan divine, Henry Burton was appointed Rector. After two sermons that he preached in 1636 in which he charged the bishops with popish innovations and described them as being not pillars of the church but "caterpillars", Burton was put in the pillory and had his ears cut off. Further troubles arose with the Restoration of Charles II and the ejectment of the then Rector for his refusal to use the Book of Common Prayer in accordance with the Act of Uniformity. Pepys in his *Diary* for 24 August 1662 — the day when the Act came into force — tells of a disturbance at St Matthew's when "a great many young (people) knotting together and crying out 'porridge' (the Puritan nickname for the Prayer Book) often and seditiously in the church; and took the Common Prayer Book, they say, away; and some say did tear it". After being destroyed in the Great Fire, the church was rebuilt by Wren in 1685. Being

one of the least expensive of his churches, it was, Hatton remarks, "very plain". He notes, however, the "finely-carved" pulpit which, together with the font and cover from St Matthew's are now at St Andrew by the Wardrobe. Hatton also mentions adornments to the reredos, now to be seen built into the hall of the mansion at Polesden Lacey near Dorking. Also surviving from St Matthew's, after it was pulled down in 1885, are several monuments in the north aisle of St Vedast Church Foster Lane, with which the parish had already been united — one being to "Mr John Cole, Tobacconist, Citizen and Founder formerly of Wood Street". Parish boundary marks can be found on the south side of Cheapside.

55. ST MICHAEL BASSISHAW

St Michael Bassishaw, which was founded around 1141 and situated on the west side of Basinghall Street, was so named from the Basing family who, in medieval times, owned a great house here known as "Basing's Hall". Records shown that William, a fourteenth-century parish priest, was involved in a dispute with the civic authorities. To endeavour to prove his right of way he had dug a ditch, but was ordered to fill this in. The parish was a wealthy one, inhabited by many successful businessmen. Among them was a seventeenth-century Mercer, John Bancks, who on his death left money for the purchase of two Communion flagons to be inscribed with his motto: "Think and thank God". One of these was for St Michael Bassishaw, the parish where Bancks died, and is now on display in St Paul's Cathedral Treasury. The Restoration ushered in a sad chapter for St Michael's. Francis Hall, a chaplain to Charles II, was appointed Rector in 1662 and, like others, also held a country benefice. Immediately the Great Plague broke out, Hall forsook this London parish for the latter, not returning until 1670 — and then only to claim his dues when the tithe was inaugurated, much to the disgust of his City parishioners. To add to this unhappy story, a priest named Phillips, who took charge of St Michael's during its Rector's absence, died of the Plague together with his wife and their three children in September 1665. It was thus left to the Vestry and churchwardens to do their best for the parish — particularly after the church was destroyed in the Great Fire the following year. Thanks to their efforts St Michael Bassishaw was rebuilt by Wren and completed in 1679, by which time Francis Hall had mercifully resigned. Nevertheless, due to the weakness of its foundations the Wren building was closed in the early 1890s, the parish later being united with that of St Lawrence Jewry. During the course of demolition a section of the tower was found at the west end dating from the fifteenth century when the rebuilding of the pre-Fire church was known to have taken place. A City Corporation plaque on the steps leading to the Guildhall entrance marks the site of St Michael's which, it says, was "demolished 1900". The weather-vane that was originally made for St Michael Bassishaw in 1712 by Andrew Niblett, a coppersmith, costing £79.16s.0d., and which after the church's demolition had various wanderings, including a sojourn in a former Lord Mayor's garden, can now be seen adorning the tower of St Andrew by the Wardrobe.

56. ST MICHAEL CROOKED LANE

First mentioned in 1270 or 1271, St Michael's was considerably enlarged about a century later, when a college of priests to serve the church was founded by the distinguished Mayor and Fishmonger, Sir William Walworth. Stow describes it as "this fair church", but adds that most of the south side was destroyed by an explosion caused by a stranger imprudently firing a gun, which then burst a store of gunpowder in a house in Crooked Lane. Weaver, in *Ancient Funeral Monuments*, published in 1631, records this epitaph on a monument in St Michael's:

> "Here lyeth wrapt in clay
> The body of William Wray
> I have no more to say".

It was in Crooked Lane within St Michael's parish that the first deaths in the City from the Great Plague occurred in 1665. The church was destroyed in the Fire of the following year. It was rebuilt by Wren in 1687, though its handsome spire was not completed until later. The churchwardens' accounts state that in May 1773 the sum of £2.12s.6d. was paid for one "large oyl cloth umbrella" to be used at burials in bad weather, as had been ordered at a previous meeting of the Vestry. A famous building in the parish was the Boar's Head Tavern. This, like St Michael's church itself, was demolished in order to make way for the approaches to the new London Bridge. According to *The Times* report, the final service took place on Sunday 20 March 1831 with a crowded congregation present. About halfway through the proceedings, alarm was caused when a quantity of mortar fell from the ceiling, while a second and larger fall compelled the service to be abruptly concluded "to the great injury of the collection for charity"! Of Crooked Lane, once famous for its bird-cages and fishing-tackle shops, the last vestiges were swept away after World War II. Boundary marks of St Michael's are on the outer archway of St Magnus the Martyr, with which the parish is united, and there is a modern window inside St Magnus depicting the church. On permanent loan to the St Paul's Treasury is the "Falstaff" cup of 1590, a gourd-shaped vessel on which, it is alleged, Sir John Falstaff swore to wed Mistress Quickly, and which was presented to the St Michael's Vestry which used to meet at the Boar's Head. And in a walled open space on the south side of St Magnus can be found a tombstone, formerly in the churchyard of St Michael Crooked lane, to Robert Preston "late Drawer at the Boar's-head Tavern in Great Eastcheap" who — says the fitting epitaph — "drew good wine (and) took care to fill his Pots", and died on 16 March 1730.

57.   ST MICHAEL QUEENHITHE

"A convenient church but all the monuments therein are defaced" is how Stow describes St Michael's Queenhithe, a building which is first mentioned in the twelfth century. Standing immediately opposite Queenhithe Dock, the church doubtless played an important role in the life of what was, in medieval days, one of London's busy ports. Destroyed in the Great Fire, it was rebuilt by Wren in 1677. Sir James Thornhill, the celebrated artist who painted the dome of St Paul's Cathedral, contributed to St Michael's: for, according to Malcolm in his *Londinium Redivivum*, the church officers returned public thanks to Sir James for his "liberality in repairing and improving the painting which adorned their altar" in 1721. Malcolm also notes that there were then many sugar houses in this neighbourhood. One reminder of this may have been Sugar Loaf Court, which existed in Queenhithe Ward until the changes that occurred after World War II. In contrast to many of the Wren churches which were almost completely concealed behind warehouses and business premises, St Michael's possessed an impressive south frontage facing Queenhithe. In spite of this, the building was demolished in 1876 and the parish united with that of St James Garlickhithe. The choir stalls from St Michael's and the pulpit — complete with a wooden peg on which the preacher could hang his wig on hot days — went to St James's where they are still to be seen. The font found a home in St Michael's Camden Town, which was built out of the proceeds from the sale of its namesake in Queenhithe. A particularly

interesting survival is the vane on Cole Abbey Church (formerly St Nicholas Cole Abbey), in Queen Victoria Street. This is known to have been restored in 1770, but dates from considerably earlier, and is a model of one of the corn-ships that would have docked at Queenhithe in bygone days. Beneath it is a ball, reputed to be capable of containing an exact bushel of grain; yet another allusion to the trade in corn which once flourished in this area and may even have given Queenhithe its name. A parish boundary mark can be seen on the Royal Bank of Canada Centre in Little Trinity Lane.

58.   ST MICHAEL WOOD STREET

"A proper thing, and lately well repaired" is Stow's description of St Michael's Church which stood on the west side of Wood Street and on the corner of Huggin Lane and is first mentioned in the reign of Richard I. It is to Stow that we owe the intriguing story of how, following the battle of Flodden Field, the body of the Scottish King James IV was taken to Sheen Monastery in Surrey, and after the dissolution of the religious houses in Henry VIII's reign it was thrown out among rubble. According to Stow "workmen there for their foolish pleasure hewed off his head" and this eventually came to be buried in St Michael's Wood Street. Although the church suffered much damage in the Great Fire, the medieval stone walls remained standing, so that protected by a temporary roof the parishioners continued to worship there. The parochial records testify to the concern of the churchwardens over the matter of rebuilding. Thus in 1671 they paid £15.15s.0d. "for a dinner for Dr Wren and other charges" and two years later they persuaded the architect to accompany them "to a church in Lumber Street" to compare the arrangements there for rebuilding. Even so, St Michael's was among Wren's least expensive churches, with a tower surmounted by a turret and internally very plain. This, however, gave no excuse for the Victorian vandalism which occurred in 1887–88, when, to replace high pews, there were installed yellow deal benches and chancel stalls of the same material with "Gothick" ends and the organ lost its carved case. Some years earlier, a poor spire had been substituted for the Wren turret. Hence, when it was decided to demolish St Michael's in 1894 and to unite the parish with that of St Alban Wood Street, no case could be argued for its preservation on grounds of architectural merit. Huggin Lane has been swallowed up in post-war rebuilding and the site of St Michael's Wood Street has completely vanished. Of the few furnishing which survived nineteenth-century vandalism, paintings of Moses and Aaron can be seen in the reredos of St Anne and St Agnes Gresham Street. Guildhall Library has registers of St Michael's from the mid-sixteenth century and vestry minutes and churchwardens' accounts from the seventeenth century, though they are incomplete.

59.   **ST MILDRED POULTRY**

Centred in the busy Poultry market, St Mildred's would have been a lively and colourful parish in the medieval City. Although not mentioned until 1175, the dedication to a Saxon saint who founded a Kentish religious house of which she became Abbess, suggests an earlier foundation. Among those buried in the pre-Fire church was the sixteenth-century agricultural writer Thomas Tusser, author of a book entitled *Five Hundred Points of Good Husbandry*. He unhappily engaged in ruinous speculations resulting in his imprisonment in the Poultry Compter for debt. He died there and on 9 May 1580 was buried in St Mildred's, the epitaph on his grave being, according to Stow:

> "Here Thomas Tusser clad in earth doth lie,
> That sometimes made the points of husbandry,
> By him then learn thou mayest, here learn we must,
> When all is done we sleep and turn to dust,
> And yet through Christ to heaven we hope to go:
> Who reads his books shall find his faith was so".

Some idea of the effects of the Plague and Fire on the parish may be gained from the registers for 1667 and 1668 which have only eight names — all burials — and this note:

"What from the Wasting Plague and Dreadfull Fire, the Parishioners were dispersed and so no Entries made". Nor were the parishioners of the nearby St Mary Colechurch keen, after the Fire, to be associated with St Mildred's which they described as "perpetually disturbed with the noises of carts and coaches, and wants sufficient place for burials". According to Thomas Milbourn, the interior of the church rebuilt by Wren was "plain but lofty and well lighted". He drew particular attention to its pulpit with a curiously-carved representation of a ship in full sail on its front panel. This and a similar emblem on the tower-vane were said to be reminders of the part played by the patron St Mildred in encouraging trade and navigation. Changes in the City's resident population in the nineteenth century meant that fewer people lived in the parish or attended services. An article in *The Times* of December 6 1871 indicates that the church had finally closed the previous week; while a letter from the Vestry Clerk a week later said that with the church occupying so prominent a position, the scantiness of its congregation had become a disgrace and a byword. Furthermore, the building had impeded the widening of the Poultry which took place after its demolition. From the proceeds of its sale St Paul's Goswell Road was built, and some furniture, including the pulpit with ship, was transferred there — only to be destroyed in World War II. The ship on the vane was more fortunate, going to adorn St Olave Jewry with which St Mildred's was united. It can still be seen on St Olave's tower in Ironmonger Lane, while a City Corporation plaque in Poultry marks the spot where St Mildred's stood.

60. **ST OLAVE JEWRY**
The name Old Jewry, the street on the west side of which stood St Olave's church, carries the reminder of a less enlightened aspect of medieval London life, when this area of the City was a ghetto where Jews were forced to live. The church's other name of St Olave Upwell, found in old records and due to the existence in the churchyard of a well which used to provide excellent water, presents a more pleasing picture. First mentioned in the twelfth century, St Olave's is referred to by Stow as "a proper parish church". The vestry minutes of 1589 mention "sluggishness and divers unreverend behaviour" on the part of servants and children during service-time — an indication of the unattractiveness of the Established Church in the Elizabethan age. Destroyed in the Great Fire, St Olave Jewry was rebuilt by Wren during the period 1673–76. Among eighteenth-century worshippers was Alderman John Boydell, the well-known engraver and print-publisher, and donor of many paintings to the City Corporation, who lived in Cheapside on the corner of Ironmonger Lane. Boydell was clearly "a character". Each morning at 5 o'clock he would make his way up Ironmonger Lane to Church Court — now St Olave's Court — and, having placed his wig on the ball on the top of the pump there, would sluice his head in the water under its spout. A monument to Boydell, erected in St Olave's after his burial, is now in St Margaret Lothbury which became the church of the united parishes following the closure of St Olave Jewry in 1888. The site was auctioned for development in July 1891, but the tower was spared and, topped by the sailing-ship weather vane from St Mildred Poultry, it serves both as offices and as a residence for St Margaret's Rector. Altar-rails formerly in St Olave Jewry were used to construct the screen of the chapel

in St Margaret's, while other furnishings went to the newly-built church of St Olave Woodberry Down. Between October 1985 and June 1986 excavations undertaken by members of the Museum of London Department of Archaeology at St Olave's Court revealed the remains of the founda-tions of a late Saxon church, dated between the ninth and eleventh cen-turies, and containing Roman tiles.

61. ST PETER LE POER

This church, first mentioned in 1181, was situated on the west side of Old Broad Street close to where is now the arch leading to Austin Friars. According to Stow it was "so called for a difference from others of that name, sometime peradventure a poor parish, but at the present time there be many fair houses, possessed by rich merchants and others". One finds it hard to imagine the inhabitants of Old Broad Street as ever suffering from poverty and it should be said that Stow's derivation has been questioned. Between 1629 and 1631 the steeple and a costly gallery at the west end were newly built. The Rector at that time was Richard Holdsworth who became a noted preacher and was appointed Gresham Professor of Divinity. Although a moderate Puritan, Holdsworth was a staunch churchman and supporter of Charles I. This, and his refusal to take the oath to the Solemn League and Covenant, resulted in his imprisonment in the Tower in 1643. A Rector of a very different standpoint was the eighteenth-century Latitudinarian, Benjamin Hoadly, later Bishop of Bangor and then of Winchester. It was while at St Peter le Poer that Hoadly put forward those theological opinions which caused such offence to High Churchmen of the time and led to what became known as the Bangorian Controversy. The church narrowly escaped the Great Fire, the flames of which, as Hatton remarks, almost reached the west end. Incidentally, Hatton comments unfavourably on the dust which made the tables of the Lord's Prayer and Creed illegible. By the end of the eighteenth century extensive repairs had become necessary, and the opportunity was taken to rebuild the church

further back from the street so as to ease traffic problems. Jesse Gibson, whose portrait hangs in Drapers' Hall (of which he was Surveyor), was the architect chosen for the task, and he completed it in 1792. Opinions differ as to the merits of the building: a fair assessment would seem to be that it "was not a particularly interesting example of a centrally planned church". According to *The Times* of July 3 1907, the sale of the disused church of St Peter and its site had then just taken place, though the City Corporation had already secured a strip of the frontage for street-widening. The conditions were that the building should be pulled down within two months of the completion of purchase, the parish having been united with that of St Michael Cornhill. The pulpit, font and panelling found their way to St Peter le Poer Friern Barnet, a new church built with money from the sale of that in the City. Of the latter no trace remains other than parish boundary marks in Throgmorton Avenue.

(The church of Holy Trinity Minories has not been included here, since, despite the fact that its parish is now united with that of St Botolph Aldgate, it was outside the City boundaries. Furthermore, although its registers are in Guildhall Library, the vestry minutes are kept at Mile End, and the churchwardens' accounts at Lambeth.)

III
Churches Destroyed in World War II and Not Rebuilt in the City

Margaret Whinney, in her book Wren, *has remarked that with possibly the exception of Coventry Cathedral, the destruction of the City churches was the heaviest architectural loss suffered by Britain in World War II. Few of them entirely escaped damage during the air-raids of 1940 and 1941, and twenty were reduced to shells. But it is with those which more or less completely vanished that we are concerned in this third and last section. Much heart-searching must have taken place as to which buildings should or should not be restored. For years there had been talk of "too many City churches" and reckless decisions then could easily have resulted in their number being drastically reduced. It must never be forgotten that the City churches are not only Grade I listed buildings, they are also places of prayer and worship, valued and used by many of the thousands of commuters who pour into the "Square Mile" from Monday to Friday of each week. Ultimately, three Wren churches: St Mildred Bread Street, St Stephen Coleman Street and St Swithin London Stone vanished altogether; the towers alone of four: St Alban Wood Street, St Augustine Watling Street, Christ Church Greyfriars and St Dunstan in the East were restored and preserved; and the stones of one: St Mary the Virgin Aldermanbury, were carefully dismantled and transferred to the United States where, rebuilt and rehallowed, St Mary's now serves as a unique chapel for Westminster College, Fulton, Missouri.*

62. **CHRIST CHURCH GREYFRIARS**

When, in the late 1220s, the Franciscans — known from the habit they wore as "Grey Friars" — arrived in London, they deliberately chose for their dwelling a site near Newgate which, as the names Stinking Lane and Shambles suggest, was particularly unpleasant. Later, following the consecration of their magnificent church (some 300 feet long), their manner of life changed; especially when this building became renowned for the number of eminent and wealthy people buried there — it has been remarked that the list resembled *Burke's Peerage*! With the dissolution of the religious houses under Henry VIII, the monuments in Greyfriars were either removed or defaced. In 1547 the church was refounded as the parish church of Christ Church, incorporating the former parishes of St Nicholas Shambles and St Ewin. Edward VI granted the Foundation Charter of what replaced Greyfriars and became known as

"Christ's Hospital", the celebrated school whose pupils still wear the Tudor dress with dark blue coat and yellow stockings. Until 1666, they used the old Franciscan church for their worship. Then came the Great Fire, which caused considerable destruction, although it is recorded that the glazed windows were "very little damnified". The church built by Wren between 1684 and 1704 was one of his largest, even though it occupied what had formed the quire in its predecessor. Among burials in the restored building was that of Richard Baxter, the distinguished Nonconformist divine, on December 17 1691. It possessed some good fittings, to which was added in the nine-teenth century a fine hexagonal pulpit from the Temple Church. On the Renatus Harris organ Mendelssohn played. To accommodate the Christ's Hospital boys were galleries, described as "desperately uncomfortable", and so constructed that the boys were unable to kneel. Pearce, in *Annals of Christ's Hospital*, quotes from the records an entry dated September 30 1737, referring to "the irregular and Disorderly singing of the Children in Christ Church to the great interruption and disturbance of the Congregation". Nevertheless, one of the best-known Blue Coat scholars, Charles Lamb, described the Christ's Hospital boy as a "religious character". Moreover, there seems to have been a sense of regret when, in 1902, the school was moved to Horsham. For as long as Christ Church remained, some 300 pupils used to come up to the City to attend service every St Matthew's Day. They still come, but now have to go elsewhere: for, with the exception of its tower and ruined nave, Christ Church is no more. Not only did the building perish during the bombing of 1940 and 1941, but also many of the precious records. However, the tower survived, and with the spire which was restored in 1960 with the addition of urns replacing those removed in the nineteenth century, presents a splendid appearance. The City Corporation has set up a board in the garden at the corner of King Edward Street, with details of the history of the building and the work done since World War II. The rebuilt Vestry House in Greyfriars Passage replaces that of 1760.

63. **ST ALBAN WOOD STREET**

"What is that?" is a question often asked by people when they see the tower of the former Wren church of St Alban standing in isolation in the middle of Wood Street, and without any indication whatever as to its past history or even its name. According to Professor W.F. Grimes, who was responsible for excavations carried out in 1961–62, the earliest religious building on this site was "Saxon and at least of eighth-ninth century date", and presumably a chapel attached to the neighbouring palace of King Offa. During the twelfth century Offa's chapel became the parish church of St Alban in Wood Street. Stow lists various monuments to distinguished citizens buried there, including one to Sir John Cheke, tutor to the young King Edward VI. Anthony Munday, who continued the *Survey of London* down to the 1630s, noted the importance of the church's dedication to the first British martyr, and commented on its antique arches and pillars. He also mentioned Roman bricks as being incorpo-rated in the building and refers to a tower which he believed to be part of Offa's palace in the nearby Love Lane. During the 1630s the celebrated architect Inigo Jones is said to have redesigned St Alban's, and some of his building evidently survived the

Great Fire and was used in the church of 1682–87 which Wren built in the Gothic style. This contained good seventeenth-century fittings, some of which were replaced during the Victorian period by Sir George Gilbert Scott, who made what he regarded as "improvements", including an apse in place of the old east window. While these were accepted, there does appear to have been a protest when sometime later the parapet and pinnacles of the tower were renewed, but in a darker stone. On Sunday 29 December 1940 almost all of St Alban's — including a granite fountain in its churchyard bearing the simple inscription "The gift of A.M. Silber 1875" — was destroyed during one of the worst raids on the City. However, Wren's tower survived, and this has been restored and preserved as an historic landmark, while at the same time providing unusual residential and business accommodation. It would have been pleasing to be able to direct the reader to St Vedast Foster Lane to see there a rare hourglass in its frame which was rescued from the burnt-out St Alban's. Sad to say, this has latterly disappeared — and no one knows where.

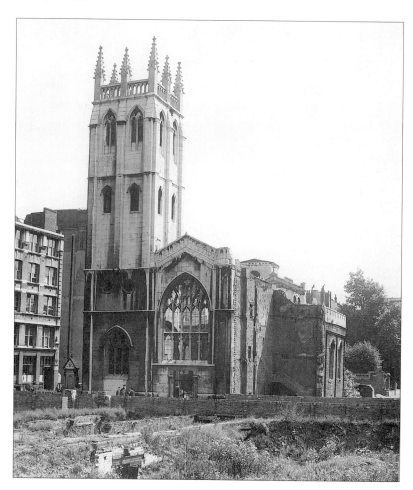

64.   **ST AUGUSTINE WATLING STREET**

Named after Augustine of Canterbury, this church stood only a short distance away from one dedicated to Gregory the Great, who had been responsible for sending Augustine on his evangelistic mission to England during the sixth century. Both churches were destroyed in the Great Fire, but only St Augustine's was rebuilt, the main part being completed by Wren in 1683, though its steeple was not finished until 1695. Originally, it was known as St Augustine "ad Portam" from its proximity to a gate leading to the Cathedral precincts. Until World War II it stood on the corner of Watling Street and Old Change, but is now separated from the former by New Change; while Old Change, which was so called from the King's Exchange once situated there, has entirely disappeared. The list of Rectors dated back to 1148 and included R.H. Barham, author of *The Ingoldsby Legends*, who was there from 1842 until his death three years later. Particularly noteworthy is Daniel Waterland, described as "one of the most learned and effective champions of Anglican orthodoxy in the eighteenth century", who was Rector from 1721 to 1730 and during that time published

his important *Critical History of the Athanasian Creed*. Alterations carried out to the church in the late nineteenth century, which included the removal of the south and west galleries, are said to have taken away some of the building's charm. A new chapter began in the history of the church when Henry Ross was inducted as Rector in 1936. A well-known Anglo-Catholic priest, who had previously been Vicar of St Alban's Holborn, he attracted considerable congregations at the daily services which he introduced and especially at the Sunday Eucharist where there grew up a fine musical tradition. Unfortunately, this was to be of comparatively short duration. Among the manuscripts in Guildhall Library may be found a Service Register of St Augustine's which, although scorched and partially burnt during the blitz, contains a precious record set down in the Rector's own handwriting. So, early in 1941, we read:"Alas. Sad to state this church was bombed, burnt out and utterly demolished on Saturday night and Sunday Jan. 11–12 by the Nazi enemy". Nevertheless, two days later, weekday services were resumed in the Vestry, with the Sunday Eucharist at St Martin Ludgate. Then, on Sunday 10 May, is this sad note: "Ghastly raid all night. Vestry gone; tower gone; everything burnt out, nothing left". But within less than two months on Tuesday 1 July the Rector writes: "Holy Communion in St Augustine's Tower Chapel opened today" — and from then on weekday services were held until the parish was finally transferred to St Mary le Bow in 1954. After the Fire of 1666, the parish of St Faith under St Paul's was united with St Augustine's, and when during the blitz a cat was discovered in the tower of the latter, refusing to abandon the kittens to whom she had given birth, the Rector appropriately named her "Faith". The diocesan authorities at first planned to utilise the church site for the erection of a Cathedral Chapter House, but eventually it became incorporated in the new St Paul's Choir School, the tower being restored and given a fibre-glass replica of Wren's original spire. The processional cross formerly belonging to St Augustine's is now kept in the Dean's aisle of St Paul's and can be seen in regular use at the Cathedral services.

65.   ST DUNSTAN IN THE EAST

"Juxta Turrim" — next to, or near, the Tower — is how St Dunstan's was referred to in old documents. Later, it was described as "in the East" to distinguish it from the church dedicated to the same saint in Fleet Street. Stow speaks of it in his *Survey* as "a fair and large church of an ancient building, and within a large churchyard". In his *Annals* he mentions "a fearful fray" which occurred in St Dunstan's on the afternoon of Easter Day 1417, when many were severely wounded and one "slain out of hand", which caused the church to be closed for some time. There still exist parish records from the end of the fifteenth century, although the "Great Book", dating back to 1300, appears to have been lost in the Fire of 1666. Samuel Pepys refers to St Dunstan's several

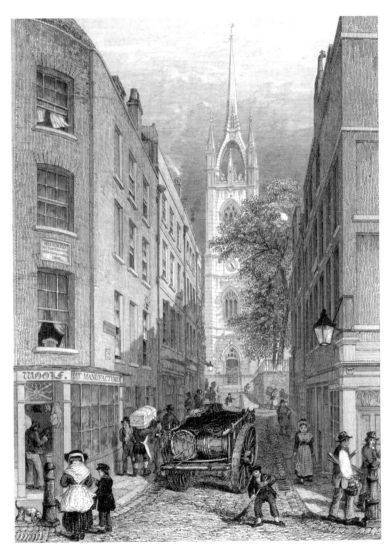

times in his *Diary*. He notes how in July 1665, when the Great Plague was at its height, Admiral Sir John Lawson was buried there late at night "without any company at all". And while on Sunday 9 August 1663 he had heard an excellent sermon by George Gifford, the Rector, on the text "Remember Lot's wife". A less pleasant experience occurred in April 1668 when, on his way home, as he was entering the ruins at St Dunstan's, he "was met by two rogues with clubs" and narrowly escaped what today would be called "a mugging". Old prints of the City before 1666 show the leaden steeple of St Dunstan's towering above most others in the "Square Mile". Then, in what the church records describe as the "dismal fire", it was seen tottering and gradually falling to the ground. When Wren undertook the church's restoration, he paid particular attention to the tower and spire which, tradition says, was designed by his daughter. Built in the Gothic style with arches and flying buttresses, reminding one of St Nicholas Newcastle-upon-Tyne, it was among the architect's masterpieces. Seemingly delicate, its strength was such that when, after the Great Storm of 1703, Wren was told that some of his spires had suffered damage, he replied "Not St Dunstan's I am sure". Nevertheless the rest of the church was less secure and during the early 1800s began to show signs of collapsing, so that David Laing, architect of the nearby Custom House, was entrusted with the work of its rebuilding. In the late nineteenth century, a portion of the parochial funds was used for St Dunstan's College, Catford, in south London, and from then on, as long as the church survived there was a close link with the school. In the post-war replanning, the diocesan authorities decided that the parish should be joined to All Hallows by the Tower and the restored St Dunstan's tower be set aside for the use of the Vicar of the united parishes. Within the ruins of St Dunstan's there is today one of the most attractive oases within the City, filled on a sunny lunch-time by workers from nearby offices. According to a plaque at the east corner of St Dunstan's Alley the church was destroyed by enemy action in 1941, the garden being created by the Corporation of London and opened by the Lord Mayor on 21 June 1971. But to hear the bells of St Dunstan's one must travel to the USA where, instead of summoning people as they once did to the Eucharist, they now ring out over a Californian valley where wine is prepared. Hopefully, a little of that wine may find a place on the altar of some church there!

66. ST MARY THE VIRGIN ALDERMANBURY

Some sixty years ago, J.M.N. Jeffries could say to his readers: "Go to Aldermanbury on a Summer Sunday. Walk there and rest from your walk on a bench in the churchyard which is the church garden". Aldermanbury, though much changed, is still there, as is a garden with benches on which one can sit; but to see what the writer then likened to "a village church" one must journey many miles. The earliest mention of St Mary Aldermanbury occurs in 1181. Yet what seems to have interested Stow was not the antiquity of the church but the huge shin-bone of a man which hung in the cloister. He did, however, refer to the benefaction of William Eastfield, who was Mayor in 1438, particularly his building of the steeple and replacement of the old bells with fine "tunable" ones. Among those "eccentrics" who have added colour to the life of the Church generally, should surely be included the Scot,

mentioned by Pendrill in *Old Parish Life in London*. On June 29, 1588, he preached in St Mary's "with a kerchief on his head, a velvet nightcap upon that, and a felt hat over that, and prayed a long prayer with all on". Two notable sixteenth-century parishioners were John Heminge and Henry Condell, the personal friends of William Shakespeare. It was they who collected his writings and edited the First Folio of his plays, as their monument in the garden, surmounted by Shakespeare's bust and now a century old, testifies. Edmund Calamy became incumbent of St Mary's in 1639 and attracted large congregations. The attendance at his weekday lectures, when there were seldom fewer than sixty coaches, must have caused congestion in Aldermanbury. Nevertheless, Calamy's refusal to accept the 1662 Act of Uniformity led to his being ejected. The church was destroyed in 1666 and rebuilt by Wren. Judge Jeffreys, infamous for his savagery after Monmouth's rebellion, was at one time a parishioner. Some years after his death in the Tower, his remains were transferred to a vault in St Mary's and a plaque was set up bearing the appropriate epitaph: "The Lord seeth not as man seeth". During the nineteenth century the church suffered at the hands of Victorian "improvers" who introduced a stone reredos and pulpit. Fortunately, the replacement of these in the early years of the twentieth century by oak fittings from the demolished church of St Alphage London Wall helped to restore a Wren-like appearance. On the night of 29 December 1940, St Mary's was almost gutted in a fire-raid, though the tower and some columns survived. It was subsequently decided to unite the parish with St Vedast Foster Lane. In the early 1960s the leaders of Westminster College, Fulton, Missouri, negotiated to secure the remains of the fabric, so that a church rebuilt according to Wren's design could be erected to the memory of Sir Winston Churchill on the College campus. After their removal in 1966, the garden in Aldermanbury, to which many City workers and others go, was created. It contains a plaque with a picture of the church, now splendidly restored in America, and once again in use.

67.   ST MILDRED BREAD STREET

On the east side of the short section of Bread Street between Cannon Street and Queen Victoria Street, there stood the church of St Mildred. Almost totally destroyed during the bombing of 1941, the loss of this, one of the finest and least altered of the Wren churches, was particularly grievous. Although dedicated to a Saxon saint, the earliest reference to the church occurs in the thirteenth century. Stow mentions Lord Trenchaunt of St Alban's as supposedly being "either the new builder of this church, or best benefactor to the work thereof". Sir Nicholas Crisp, a devoted supporter of Charles I, was closely associated with St Mildred's and presented it with two silver Communion flagons. During the Great Fire the churchwardens paid twelve shillings for a coach to carry these and other items to Hackney for safety. When Sir Nicholas died in February 1665/66, his body was buried in the family vault at St Mildred's, but his heart was placed in a monument to Charles I which he had erected in the chapel at Hammersmith where he himself had a house. Despite severe damage to St Mildred's in the Fire of 1666, Wren seems to have been able to use the foundations and part of the walls in the rebuilding which he completed in 1683. Although most of the original registers perished through enemy action in 1941, there has been preserved this noteworthy entry in the nineteenth-century marriage register:

"(1816 December 30) Percy Bysshe Shelley, of the Parish of St Mildred Bread Street London Widower and Mary Wollstonecraft Godwin of the City of Bath Spinster Minor were married in this Church by Licence with consent of William Godwin her Father".

A worshipper at St Mildred's in the 1930s, sitting in the original pews, surrounded by exquisite wood-carving such as was to be seen in the pulpit, sounding-board, altar-rails and reredos, and enjoying the splendid music then provided, could easily have been transported back in time. Sadly all was lost, save for the lion and unicorn which

are now at St Anne and St Agnes Gresham Street. The square tower of St Mildred's on the south side managed to survive, but was later demolished. A board placed on the site by the City Corporation after the War, recording the church's destruction has gone, but there is a parish boundary mark on the Midland Bank No. 47 Cannon Street. In 1932, a memorial was unveiled on the west wall of the church in Bread Street to Admiral Arthur Phillip, a former parishioner who became the Founder and First Governor of Australia. The salvaging from the ruins of the bronze bust and plates enabled this memorial to be recreated on the wall beside the garden in front of No. 25 Cannon Street. It bears an inscription in which the church of St Mildred and its destruction are recorded.

68. **ST STEPHEN COLEMAN STREET**

Few who wander round the neighbourhood of Coleman Street are likely to notice on the official Ward plaques and St Stephen's parish boundary marks the small figure of an encircled cockerel. A large one in stone on a building close to where St Stephen's church formerly stood would have been lost during the demolition of the property a few years ago, had not a passer-by, seeing what was happening, ensured that it should be conveyed to the Museum of London where, if permission is obtained, it may be seen. This commemorates the bequest, in his Will of 1431, by John Sokelyng of his brewery called "La Cokke on the hoop" in Coleman Street to the Vicar, wardens and parishioners of Stephen's, provided they offered Mass on the anniversary of his death and those of his two wives. Certainly, with the financial help that such a benefaction must have brought to the church and parish, those concerned would be unlikely to have forgotten the "Cock on the Hoop". When Sokelyng made his bequest, St Stephen's Coleman Street was still a chapel-of-ease to the parish church of St Olave Jewry. Stow even said that it served for some period as a synagogue, but in this he was mistaken. Later, it became a parish church, of which the patronage was in the hands of the important Augustinian Priory of Butley in Suffolk until the dissolution of the religious houses under Henry VIII, when it passed to the parishioners. In time they were able to increase the value of the benefice, and so lay down condi-

tions as to the kind of incumbent they wanted, with the result that, by the early seventeenth century, St Stephen's had become a leading Puritan stronghold in the City. John Davenport, appointed Vicar in 1624, was frequently in trouble with the authorities, until he resigned and became a Nonconformist. His successor, John Goodwin, an even more prominent Puritan preacher, was also for a while an independent pastor. Such was the growth of radicalism among the poor inhabitants of the alleys off Coleman Street that some modern writers have described the parish as "the 'Faubourg St Antoine' of the English Revolution". Anthony Munday, who continued Stow's *Survey*, was buried in the pre-Fire church on August 9 1633. Destroyed in 1666, St Stephen's was rebuilt by Wren between 1674 and 1681. Notable seventeenth-century furnishings included a magnificent Communion-table, supported at the angles by four large carved eagles and two cherubs in the centre. Its loss during World War II was grievous, as was also that of a wood-carving of the Last Judgement originally over the entrance-gate, but, ironically, at some earlier date removed to the Vestry for safety. A replica survived and is now in the Museum of London's reserve store. The various activities which caused St Stephen's to thrive during the 1930s were all bought to an end when the church was destroyed by bombs. Nothing now marks its former site on the west side of Coleman Street between Gresham Street and Mason's Avenue.

69.   ST SWITHIN LONDON STONE

The earliest reference to the church of St Swithin alludes to its situation as "Candlewright" or "Candlewick" Street where, in medieval times, those who made candles and wicks for household purposes lived — "Cannon" Street is a corrupt form of the old name. Stow says that John Heende, Draper and Mayor, newly built the church in 1420, but at the time he was writing, Heende's monument had been defaced "save only his arms in the glass windows". Of seventeenth-century Rectors, one Robert Cooke preached a sermon in 1629 with the intriguing title of *A White Sheet or a Warning for whoremongers*; while another, Richard Owen, was ejected during the Interregnum for supporting the Royalist cause, but frequently ministered in the home of John Evelyn and so appears in the pages of the latter's *Diary*. The registers of St Swithin's reveal that in December 1663, the poet John Dryden was married there by licence to Lady Elizabeth Howard. In the reconstruction of the church after the Great Fire, Wren was able to make use of materials from the ruins of St Mary Bothaw, a parish which was then joined to St Swithin's. Among monuments in the rebuilt church was one to Michael Godfrey, Deputy Governor of the Bank of England who, while visiting William III during the siege of Namur, was accidentally killed by a cannon-ball. Already by Stow's time, St Swithin's had become known as "by London Stone". Strype in his edition of the *Survey* of 1720, refers to this as a great stone pitched upright on the south side of Cannon Street, "fixed in the ground very deep, fastened with bars of iron, and otherwise so strongly set, that if carts do run against it through negligence, the wheels are broken, and the stone itself unshaken". Nevertheless, the fact that at a Vestry held in May 1742 it was ordered "that the Stone commonly call'd London Stone be remov'd and plac'd against the Church, according to the Church Wardens Discretion" and that subsequently the

Mason was paid twelve shillings for removing it, shows the concern felt for the stone's safety. It was doubtless to give it greater security that, as the inscription on the plaque above says, the stone was built into the south wall of the church in 1798. Until recently, it was believed that London Stone had been a Roman milestone; but post-war excavations have revealed that the Roman Governor's Palace stood on the south side of Cannon Street and that the stone is probably a relic of that building. When it was eventually decided that the church should not be rebuilt after its destruction in World War II, the condition was laid down that London Stone must be incorporated in the new building to be erected on the site. St Swithin's is remembered in the name of the lane which runs alongside what was the church's east end and those who penetrate Salters Hall Court as far as Oxford Court will be rewarded with the sight of a little oasis complete with seats and known as St Swithin's Church Garden. The seventeenth-century pulpit, which was saved from destruction during the War, is now at All Hallows by the Tower.

BIBLIOGRAPHY

Use has been made of the fine collection of manuscripts, particularly vestry minutes and churchwardens' accounts, in Guildhall Library, and of printed material on individual churches kept there. The diaries of Samuel Pepys and John Evelyn have also been consulted. In addition the following works may be mentioned:

Amery, C.	*Wren's London* (Lennard, Luton, 1988)
Bell, W.G.	*The Great Plague in London in 1665* (2nd edit. Lane, London, 1951)
Bell, W.G.	*The Great Fire of London in 1666* (3rd edit. Lane, London, 1923)
Blatch, M.	*A Guide to London's Churches* (Constable, London, 1978)
Cobb, G.	*The Old Churches of London* (3rd edit. Batsford, London, 1948)
Cobb, G.	*London City Churches* (new edit. by N. Redman, Batsford, London, 1989)
Cox, J.C.	*Churchwardens' Accounts* (Antiquary's Books, Methuen, London, 1913)
Grimes, W.F.	*The Excavation of Roman and Medieval London* (Routledge & Kegan Paul, London, 1968)
Harben, H.A.	*A Dictionary of London* (Jenkins, London, 1918)
Hatton, E.	*A New View of London* (J. Nicholson, London, 1708, 2 vols.)
Hauer, C.E. Jr. & Young, W.A.	*A Comprehensive History of the London Church and Parish of St Mary the Virgin, Aldermanbury* (The Edwin Mellen Press, Lampeter, 1994)
Hennessy, G.	*Novum repertorium ecclesiasticum parochiale Londinense* (Swan Sonnenschein, London, 1898)
Huelin, G.	*The Pre-Fire City Churches* (St Margaret Pattens, London, 1968)
Huelin, G.	*Think and thank God* (The Mercers' Company, London, 1993)
Jeffries, J.M.N.	*London and Better* (Hutchinson, London, 1936)
Kent, W.	*The Lost Treasures of London* (Phoenix House Ltd., London, 1947)
Machyn, H.	*The Diary of Henry Machyn* (edited by J.G. Nichols, Camden Society, London, 1848)
Malcolm, J.P.	*Londinium Redivivum* (Rivington, London, 1803–07, 4 vols.)
Milbourn, T.	*The History of the Church of St Mildred the Virgin, Poultry* (J.R. Smith, London, 1872)
Newcourt, R.	*Repertorium ecclesiasticum parochiale Londinense* (Bateman, London, 1708–10, 2 vols.)
Pearce, E.H.	*Annals of Christ's Hospital* (2nd edit. Hugh Rees, London, 1908)
Pendrill, C.	*Old Parish Life in London* (Oxford Univ. Press, London, 1937)
RCHM	*Royal Commission on Historical Monuments, London IV: City* (H.M.S.O., London, 1929)
Riley, H.T.	*Memorials of London and London Life in the XIIIth, XIVth and XVth centuries* (Longmans, London, 1868)

Schofield, J.	*The London Surveys of Ralph Treswell* (London Topographical Society, Pubn. 135, London, 1987)
Schofield, J.	*The Building of London, from the Conquest to the Great Fire* (rev. edit. British Museum Press, London, 1993)
Stow, John	*A Survey of London* (with Introduction and Notes by C.L. Kingsford, Clarendon Press, Oxford, 1908, 2 vols.)
Torry, G.	*The Book of Queenhithe* (Barracuda Books, Buckingham, 1979)
Walters, H.B.	*London Churches at the Reformation* (SPCK, Church Historical Society, Pubn. 37, London, 1939)
Weinreb, B. & Hibbert C. (eds.)	*The London Encyclopaedia* (Macmillan, London, 1983)

ILLUSTRATIONS

Unless otherwise stated illustrations are from Guildhall Library.

APPENDIX

Compiled by Dr Peter Galloway

Boundary Marks of Vanished City Churches

The following list does not pretend to be exhaustive; it lists only those marks which were visible in the summer of 1995 and can be seen by those who use this book as a 'walking guide' to the lost City churches. It is believed that some surviving marks are located inside buildings, and cannot be seen without permission, and these have been omitted. Given that much of the City of London has been rebuilt since the Second World War, and that much of it is still being rebuilt, or buildings given new facades, it is quite possible that some visible marks may have been inadvertently missed through being temporarily removed, or through being concealed by scaffolding. It is also sad to say that in the years ahead, some of these marks may be removed and lost, or given into the safe keeping of the Museum of London. Not every owner is proud to have an historic boundary mark displayed on the front of his building.

Those who would like to undertake a deeper study of boundary marks in the City of London should begin with the impressive and thorough survey of the subject undertaken by Mr Leonard Maguire, whose working notes on the subject, now bound in seven volumes, are located in Manuscripts Department of Guildhall Library (MS 28495).

Peter Galloway

CHURCH	DATE AND NUMBER	STREET	BUILDING
All Hallows Bread Street	1843	Watling Street	Allen and Overy Building Nos. 9–12 Cheapside
All Hallows Bread Street	1813	Cheapside	No. 46
All Hallows Bread Street	1843	Watling Court	No. 47 Cannon Street
All Hallows Honey Lane	1846	Cheapside	No. 100
All Hallows Honey Lane	1846	Cheapside	British Telecom Building

CHURCH	DATE AND NUMBER	STREET	BUILDING
All Hallows Lombard Street	1883 (numbered '2')	Lombard Court	No. 29 Gracechurch Street
All Hallows Lombard Street	1883 (numbered '1')	Gracechurch Street	No. 29
All Hallows Lombard Street	1883 (numbered '23')	Lime Street Passage	No. 38
All Hallows Lombard Street	1883 (numbered '24')	Lime Street Passage	No. 58A
All Hallows Lombard Street	1883 (numbered '26')	Lime Street Passage	20 Lime Street
All Hallows Lombard Street	1883 (numbered '10')	Lombard Street	No. 39
All Hallows Staining	1852	Billiter Street	Lloyds 51 Lime Street
All Hallows Staining	1867	Fenchurch Avenue	Lloyds 51 Lime Street
All Hallows Staining	1867	London Street	60 Fenchurch Street
All Hallows the Great	1817	Upper Thames Street	No. 80 (Walbrook Wharf)
Christ Church Greyfriars	no date	Amen Court	No. 1
Holy Trinity the Less	1878	Great St Thomas Apostle	No. 4
Holy Trinity the Less	1824	Great Trinity Lane	The Bank of Canada
St Alban Wood Street	1886	Love Lane	Barrington House 59-67 Gresham Street

CHURCH	DATE AND NUMBER	STREET	BUILDING
St Alban Wood Street	1886	Love Lane	Wood Street Police Station
St Andrew Hubbard	1888	Philpot Lane	No. 10
St Andrew Hubbard	1888	Talbot Court	No. 9
St Bartholomew by the Exchange	1796	Angel Court	No. 1
St Bartholomew by the Exchange	1796	Copthall Avenue	on the arch above the entrance to Angel Court between Nos. 1A and 1B
St Bartholomew by the Exchange	1796	Threadneedle Street	The Bank of England
St Bartholomew by the Exchange	1796	Throgmorton Street	No. 30
St Bartholomew by the Exchange	1800	corner of Lothbury and Bartholomew Lane	The Bank of England
St Benet Gracechurch	1885 (numbered '28')	Gracechurch Street	No. 51
St Benet Gracechurch	1885 (numbered '17')	Lombard Court	No. 29 Gracechurch Street
St Benet Gracechurch	1885 (numbered '10')	Lombard Court	No. 29 Gracechurch Street
St Benet Gracechurch	1885 (numbered '9')	Gracechurch Street	No. 29
St Benet Gracechurch	1885 (numbered '33')	Talbot Court	Nos. 51–54 Gracechurch Street
St Christopher le Stocks	1867	Angel Court	No. 1

CHURCH	DATE AND NUMBER	STREET	BUILDING
St Christopher le Stocks	1913	Angel Court	No. 8
St Christopher le Stocks	1968 1839	Copthall Avenue	No. 2
St Christopher le Stocks	1913	Copthall Avenue	on the arch above the entrance to Angel Court between Nos. 1A and 1B
St Christopher le Stocks	1827	Princes Street	The Bank of England
St Christopher le Stocks	1781	Threadneedle Street	The Bank of England
St Dionis Backchurch	1903	Beehive Passage	Arthur's Wine Bar
St Dionis Backchurch	1888 (numbered '49')	Fenchurch Street	No. 153
St Dionis Backchurch	1888 (numbered '21')	Leadenhall Place	8 Lime Street
St Dionis Backchurch	1888 (numbered '15')	Lime Street Passage	20 Lime Street
St Dionis Backchurch	1888 (numbered '70')	Philpot Lane	No. 10
St Faith under St Paul's	1868		On the external east wall of the cathedral
St Faith under St Paul's	1828	New Change	No. 2 St Paul's Choir School
St Gabriel Fenchurch	1900 (numbered '1')	Fenchurch Street	No. 153

CHURCH	DATE AND NUMBER	STREET	BUILDING
St George Botolph Lane	1890	Botolph Alley	No. 7
St James Duke Place	1897	Creechurch Lane	Nos. 18–20
St John the Baptist upon Walbrook	1869	Cannon Street	Walbrook House
St John the Baptist upon Walbrook	1869	Dowgate Hill	Cannon Street Station
St John the Baptist upon Walbrook	no date	College Street	Skinners' Hall
St John the Baptist upon Walbrook	1869	Walbrook	No. 17
St John the Baptist upon Walbrook	1869	Walbrook	Walbrook House
St John the Evangelist Friday Street	1890	Watling Street	Allen and Overy Building Nos. 9–12 Cheapside
St John the Evangelist Friday Street	1890	New Change	Allen and Overy Building Nos. 9–12 Cheapside
St Katherine Coleman	1863 (numbered '16')	Jewry Street	Nos. 7–17
St Katherine Coleman	1863	Lloyd's Avenue	No. 5
St Katherine Coleman	1863 (numbered '35')	London Street	60 Fenchurch Street
St Katherine Coleman	1863 (numbered '36')	London Street	60 Fenchurch Street

CHURCH	DATE AND NUMBER	STREET	BUILDING
St Katherine Coleman	1863 (numbered '14')	Northumberland Alley	No. 3 Lloyd's Avenue
St Leonard Eastcheap	1886 (numbered '10')	Gracechurch Street	No. 48
St Margaret New Fish Street	1791	Upper Thames Street	Tower of St Magnus the Martyr Church
St Martin Orgar	no date	Upper Thames Street	Tower of St Magnus the Martyr Church
St Martin Pomary	1752	Frederick's Place	No. 4A
St Martin Pomary	1879	Ironmonger Lane	Atlas House
St Martin Pomary	1752	Ironmonger Lane	No. 90 Cheapside
St Martin Pomary	1817	Ironmonger Lane	No. 20
St Martin Pomary	1817	King Street	No. 7
St Martin Pomary	1879	King Street	No. 7
St Martin Pomary	1879	King Street	No. 7
St Martin Vintry	1828	Upper Thames Street	No. 80 (Walbrook Wharf)
St Mary Bothaw	1867	Cannon Street	No. 78
St Mary Bothaw	1867	Cannon Street	Walbrook House
St Mary Bothaw	1867	Dowgate Hill	No. 17
St Mary Bothaw	1850	Oxford Court	rear of 101 Cannon Street
St Mary Colechurch	1690	Ironmonger Lane	No. 90 Cheapside
St Mary Colechurch	1789	King Street	No. 15

CHURCH	DATE AND NUMBER	STREET	BUILDING
St Mary Magdalen Milk Street	1817	Cheapside	British Telecom Building
St Mary Magdalen Milk Street	1863	Cheapside	No. 51
St Mary Magdalen Milk Street	1866	Cheapside	No. 46
St Mary Magdalen Milk Street	1857	Cheapside	No. 120
St Mary the Virgin Aldermanbury	no date	Aldermanbury	Guildhall
St Mary the Virgin Aldermanbury	no date	Aldermanbury	Barrington House 59–67 Gresham Street
St Mary the Virgin Aldermanbury	no date	Love Lane	Barrington House 59–67 Gresham Street
St Mary the Virgin Aldermanbury	no date	Love Lane	Wood Street Police Station
St Matthew Friday Street	1880	Cheapside	Nos. 40–41
St Matthew Friday Street	1880	Cheapside	Nos. 22–23
St Michael Bassishaw	1815	Basinghall Avenue	Girdlers' Hall
St Michael Bassishaw	1886	Masons' Avenue	The Old Dr Butler's Head
St Michael Bassishaw	1850	Basinghall Street	Princes House No. 95 Gresham Street
St Michael Crooked Lane	1851	Upper Thames Street	Tower of St Magnus the Martyr Church

CHURCH	DATE AND NUMBER	STREET	BUILDING
St Michael le Querne	1861	New Change	No. 2 St Paul's Choir School
St Michael Queenhithe	1861	Little Trinity Lane	The Royal Bank of Canada Centre
St Mildred Bread Street	1857	Cannon Street	No. 47
St Nicholas Acons	1853	Abchurch Lane	No. 21 Lombard Street
St Olave Jewry	1680 and 1775	Old Jewry	8 Frederick's Place
St Olave Jewry	1870	Basinghall Street	Princes House No. 95 Gresham Street
St Olave Jewry	1690 and 1775	Frederick's Place	No. 4A
St Peter Westcheap	1819	Wood Street	No. 4
St Peter Westcheap	1902	Cheapside	No. 120
St Peter Westcheap	1881	Cheapside	Nos. 40–41
St Peter le Poer	1876	Throgmorton Avenue	No. 12
St Peter le Poer	1829	Throgmorton Avenue	No. 30
St Peter le Poer	1829	Throgmorton Avenue	No. 29
St Stephen Coleman Street	1886	Basinghall Avenue	Girdlers' Hall
St Stephen Coleman Street	1913	Copthall Avenue	on the arch above the entrance to Angel Court
St Stephen Coleman Street	1968 1838	Copthall Avenue	No. 2

CHURCH	DATE AND NUMBER	STREET	BUILDING
St Stephen Coleman Street	1860	Masons' Avenue	Nos. 2–9
St Swithin London Stone	1890	Cannon Street	No. 78
St Swithin London Stone	1890	Oxford Court	rear of 103 Cannon Street
St Thomas the Apostle	1853	Great St Thomas Apostle	No. 5